In the year 1968 the Middle East needs little introduction to Christian folk. Their eyes are focused upon it from afar. Jerusalem, Jordan, Sinai, Galilee are place-names which, of late, have sounded in their ears daily. And not a few feel their hearts stirred to fulfil such prophetic exhortations as 'Pray for the peace of Jerusalem', and 'Let Jerusalem come into your mind'. If we know and appreciate Scripture as we should, imagery supplied by the Holy Land belongs to the pattern of our thought. It may well be vivified by this narrative of a tour of Jordan and Israel made as recently as May, 1967. The author gives a series of impressions made upon him by the land and its people as they appear today, touches on matters of biblical and secular history and archaeology, and, as befits the matter, is especially bent on fitting his observations into the background of the Christian Gospel. His account makes entertaining and stimulating reading, the more so as his style of narration is coloured by the scholastic world from which he has fairly recently emerged. Occasionally enthralling, it is always lively, and at the same time charged with the spiritual over-plus which brings truth home to the heart.

The cover picture of a street market in Nazareth is reproduced by kind permission of Editions Sun, Paris.

Tourist
in Israel

S. M. Houghton

The Banner of Truth Trust
78b Chiltern Street London WI

Printed and bound in Great Britain
by Hazell Watson & Viney Ltd
Aylesbury, Bucks

Contents

[5]

Introduction

SINCE Israel gained independence, renewed national status, and a part of her ancient territory in 1948, the Holy Land has been opened up to the tourist in remarkable fashion. In the past, Christians have for the most part had to visit the Land by proxy; in other words, by reading of the travels of the few who have, for one reason or another, found it possible to make the journey and grapple with the difficulties of transport in the Land itself. Latterly, however, the increased speed and ease of transport and communication, the strong desire of Israel and Jordan alike to attract tourists [chiefly as a means of revenue], and the establishing of commercial and other agencies which can negotiate arrangements of travel and accommodation so difficult for the normal person, have combined to introduce tourists into the Land in growing numbers. No longer has it been necessary to regard a visit as requiring a month or two as a minimum time. Now it can be managed by air in a fortnight, and yet give reasonable opportunity for sight-seeing from Dan to Beersheba, and even beyond.

The present writer and his wife undertook the trip by air in

May, 1967. It occupied fifteen days. All arrangements for travel and accommodation, also for tours inside the Holy Land, were made by an English Travel Agency which employed leaders of experience for the shepherding of groups of approximately thirty. The leader of the group to which we ourselves belonged was the Rev. George H. Ely, minister of a Baptist Church in North Oxford, who, with members of his family, had made the same tour in 1965. The first week was spent in Jordan, the second in Israel.

The narrative which follows is personal. As such it permits reference to all kinds of matters, some of which would be excluded from a more formal document. It also permits the recording of impressions, spiritual and otherwise. From first to last the tour was informative, enlightening and enjoyable, and the more especially so doubtless to those who loved the Lord and His Word, for many scenes which had passed before the mind's eye by way of the printed page now became vivid realities.

The chapters which follow make reference to matters historical and geographic, but they are more than a study in these subjects. They attempt some description of various parts of the Holy Land, but they also record impressions which will be an abiding memory to the narrator. If they stimulate in others an interest in the Land and its people, they will have served one of their main purposes.

It will be very soon obvious to the reader that I have little personal interest in church buildings as such. To the ecclesiastical structures associated with the holy places I give little attention. That which does not truly interest a writer cannot be expected to receive stimulating mention in his pages. I have therefore concentrated attention rather upon sites undeniably authentic, and have touched upon matters archaeological whenever they serve to throw light upon the text of Scripture. It is my hope that readers will be led to search the Scriptures and to learn increasingly the absolute veracity of 'every word that proceeds out of the mouth of God'. Palestinian topography and archaeology can be useful handmaids to theology.

The narrative was almost entirely written during the dramatic days of the Israel–Arab conflict in June, 1967. The trouble between the two peoples flared up immediately after my visit to the Holy Land ended, so that impressions received were the more strongly emphasized upon my mind and heart. To these recent events the reader will find little reference in the following pages. It is, however, a conviction underlying my own interest in Israel, that the course of this people's history is yet in a very special way being shaped by God, and that He has given promises concerning their future, both temporal and spiritual, which remain unshakably sure. 'As touching the election', runs a New Testament scripture, 'they [Israel] are beloved for the fathers' sakes, for the gifts and calling of God are without repentance': that is to say, God will never go back on His pledged word. His 'calling' which, as Handley Moule has written, 'not only invites the creature, but effects the end of the invitation', is irrevocable. Old Testament promises and New Testament prophecy, as in the eleventh chapter of *Romans*, must be fulfilled in due 'times and seasons'. The day will yet come when Israel shall be grafted back into its own olive tree. It will yet blossom and bud and fill the face of the world with fruit. 'If the casting away of them be the reconciling of the world, what shall the receiving of them be but life from the dead? If their fall be the riches of the world ... how much more their fulness? [*Romans* 11.12–15]. Israel still has a place in God's purposes, and multitudes from among that people will yet be given a part in the Church of the living God. This belief lies in the background of what is said in the following pages.

It remains to add that two of the chapters are substantially articles which I have contributed in the recent past to the *Bible League Quarterly*. They dovetail into the narrative without difficulty and furnish desirable information.

SMH

July, 1967

PATHWAYS OF THE HOLY LAND

The pathways of Thy land are little changed
  Since Thou wert there;
The busy world through other ways has ranged,
  And left these bare.

The rocky path still climbs the glowing steep
  Of Olivet,
Though rains of two millenniums wear it deep,
  Men tread it yet.

Still to the gardens o'er the brook it leads,
  Quiet and low;
Before his sheep the shepherd on it treads,
  His voice they know.

The wild fig throws broad shadows o'er it still,
  As once o'er Thee;
Peasants go home at evening up that hill
  To Bethany.

And as when gazing Thou didst weep o'er them,
  From height to height
The white roofs of discrowned Jerusalem
  Burst on our sight.

These ways were strewed with garments once, and palm,
  Which we tread thus;
Here through Thy triumph on Thou passedst, calm,
  On to Thy cross.

The waves have washed fresh sands upon the shore
  Of Galilee;
But chiselled in the hillsides evermore
  Thy paths we see.

. . . . .

And now, wherever meets Thy lowliest band
  In praise and prayer,
There is Thy presence, there Thy Holy Land,
  Thou, Thou art there!

ELIZABETH CHARLES

I

Across Europe to Asia

To a person who has never before felt the thrill of travel by air, the first such journey is an unforgettable experience. The feeling of elevation, the sensation of looking down from the skies upon scenes which hitherto have always been looked at horizontally or not at all, the knowledge that one is travelling at speeds unattainable on land, the new dimensions (so to speak) of time and space – these and much else combine to render the first trip by air the commencement of a new chapter in life, just as the conquest of the air by man introduced a new era in history. Our narrative therefore begins with some account of the flight which 'translated' us from the homeland to the Holy Land.

All preliminaries, both optional and compulsory, having been attended to, we boarded a plane at Gatwick Airport, about thirty miles south of London, on a somewhat chilly evening in early May, 1967, just as darkness was falling, and shortly after nine we found ourselves airborne. Our journey was to take place by night. As a first-ever journey by plane, I had awaited it with considerable expectancy, my chief regret being that it would in all probability be impossible to see anything worth-while of the countries over which we were scheduled to pass. France I had not seen since 1918, when the last German drive westwards in the First World War precipitated me into the area of the Somme and held me there for five months. Switzerland, Italy, and Greece were as real to me as books on history and geography could make them, but I cherished the thought of setting eyes on them for the first time during our flight.

The pages of Joseph Mazzini, Italian patriot, had assured me that the Alps were so many 'icy cherubim guarding the ap-proaches to Italy', and that their sublime grandeur reduced atheism to an impossibility. I could well believe it, for much less noble mountains bear the sure imprint of Deity. Then, too, my remembrances of what I had read in the pages of Livy in the long ago brought back clear echoes of the noise of battle in the Second Punic War. In my mind's eye I could even see Hannibal and his ponderous elephants making their incredible journey across Gaul and then across the Alps [historians still argue as to which Pass witnessed the amazing march], blasting a path through road blockages, and slithering their way down the southward-facing slopes to the Lombard Plain, and [as Livy says] to scenes more worthy of human habitation.

In Italy itself imagination had visualized the defeat of the Romans at Lake Trasimene and at Cannae, seen the Carthagin-ians yield themselves to the luxuries of Capua [was not 'Capua a Cannae to Hannibal'?], and noted their crestfallen faces at the news that, even though they occupied much of the peninsula, the very ground on which they stood was even then being pur-chased at a goodly price in the Roman forum, a transaction reminiscent of that in which Jeremiah had been involved four hundred years earlier [*Jer.* 32.6–15].

Better still, and with greater pleasure, I had [so to speak] seen

[14]

Rome's Christians journey south to Appii Forum and The Three Taverns, and witnessed their return to their world-city, not to 'welcome a conquering Caesar in', but glad at heart to have with them an apostle of Christ and the historian-physician whose praise was in all the churches. 'And so we went toward Rome'.

On the other side of the Adriatic, imagination had seen Phidippides with tireless feet make the long return journey between Athens and Sparta in little more than a couple of days, and finally fall dead of over-exertion by Athens' Acropolis as he ran back later from Marathon with the news of the defeat of the Persian hosts.

> '*The mountains look on Marathon,*
> *And Marathon looks on the sea.*'

So sang Byron, and here was my opportunity to catch a fleeting glimpse by the light of the moon of a terrain where the history of the Western world had in ancient days been decided. History, too, had shown me a Xerxes, bent on the subjugation of the restless Greeks, fleeing back to his bridge of boats at the Hellespont, and to the shelter of his Persian dominions after the defeat of his men at 'sea-born Salamis', when

> '. . . *ships by thousands lay below,*
> *And men in nations; — all were his.*
> *He counted them at break of day,*
> *And when the sun set, where were they?*'

But better by far, I had seen — dare I claim that in this case it was by faith? — the apostle of the Gentiles and his intrepid company land at Neapolis, walk the dusty highway to Philippi, sit down by a river-side, preach the Word of life, make and baptise converts, and then pass on from Macedonia to Achaia. Declaring the glad tidings of great joy destined to reach the ears of all people, they had turned the world upside down, planted churches, and 'from Jerusalem and round about unto Illyricum had fully preached the Gospel of Christ'.

And now had come the golden moment when, from the skies above, I was hoping to look down on the tangled landscape and waters of the western world, and with bounding heart see something by moonlight or even starlight of lands where the very stuff of history had been made. It was not to be. My own particular party was the last to find seats on the plane, so that I found myself sitting alongside the central corridor, all the window seats having been occupied before we mounted the gangway. We managed, however, to get an occasional glimpse of the night skies and of the terrain below, and to our joy, as we passed over Geneva, we saw the roads of Calvin's city – I refrain from saying Rousseau's – stretching like so many strings of bright beads in all directions. It was but a skeleton outline, as if a city's bones had become phosphorescent, but it was sufficient to stimulate memory. Farel, Calvin, Marian exiles [including Knox], Beza, Malan, d'Aubigné, and others of whom the world was not worthy, here lived and laboured, bequeathing to the Church of God true riches and a testimony to righteousness. The so-called Geneva Bible of Puritan fame was translated into English at this spot. Here the Scottish Robert Haldane promoted a second Reformation as he preached the doctrine of the Pauline epistles.

But air travel is speedy, and the memory of Geneva's spiritual stature was perforce fleeting. 'In ten minutes', came a voice from the cockpit of the plane, 'we shall be over Turin'. Vastly greater than Geneva in population and coverage, its lights duly appeared and we could imagine its half million inhabitants making preparations for their night's rest as we on our part settled ourselves as comfortably as might be in our adjustable seats. Soon we were cruising down the eastern coast of Italy and window passengers had glimpse after glimpse of town and village and hamlet illuminated only from below.

Few if any of us experienced any discomfort from air travel, certainly no more than is felt by 'the odd one out' in a journey by train; it is, if anything, more comfortable. An air-conditioned pressurization system works wonders. While passengers relax or read or chat or sleep, a weather-sensing and terrain-mapping radar set is scanning 150 miles ahead, seeking out weather conditions and giving the plane's captain warning of areas of turbulence and storm which may lie in his course, and this in sufficient time to avoid them by flying over or around them. Apart from an occasional bumpiness we felt nothing at all of discomfort, and certainly felt no alarm.

Here then we were, cruising aloft at 20,000 feet, and even seeking sleep as we were carried on the wings of the wind. We were aware that the roads of England which we traversed regularly were, statistically speaking, a much greater risk than airways. My wife had been impressed by a word which she passed to me in the plane. It had come to her via Daily Light and had been included in the morning portion of the day before the flight commenced: 'If I ascend up into heaven, Thou art there'. Of a certainty we had no desire to attempt a flight from the presence of the Lord. We had taken the wings of the morning and with high expectations were bound, within strict limitations, for 'the uttermost parts'; but better by far was 'the Lord God of Israel, under whose wings we had come to trust'.

Dinner about 10.30 was a pleasant interlude. A hinged tray was swivelled on to, or rather, just above our lap, and a second portable tray of slightly smaller size was placed upon it by a stewardess. Meat and vegetables, piping hot, were supplied in a container made of metal foil and about the size of a large sardine tin. Cutlery and condiments lay alongside in sealed bags. Peach slices, butter, cheese, a roll, also tea or coffee, completed the meal. Trays were then removed and the entire company of about a hundred folk relapsed into unsettled slumber.

It was no little surprise to hear the announcement at 2.30 in the morning that breakfast was about to be served. Bacon, potatoes, mushrooms, rolls and butter duly appeared under the same arrangements as before, and all of us did our sleepy best to 'lay by us in store'. A further announcement informed us, however, that by 3 o'clock we should touch down at Damascus airport for refuelling, and we had the prospects of stretching our legs and of breathing, if only for a few brief minutes, the fresh Syrian air. But our expectations were disappointed. The gangway was let down to the concrete runway of the airfield, but it was soon evident that there was to be no refuelling after all. Was it because Jordan, for which we were bound, had long been on bad terms with Syria? Somehow we got the impression that strong nationalistic feelings entered into the matter. It may be that coming events, if they were not casting their shadows before them, were at any rate deepening shadows already existing. No-one was allowed to descend the gangway except for one or two of the officers. Airport officials, glum and taciturn, were on patrol, and within ten or fifteen minutes we were airborne once again.

With sunlit skies above us and a radiant earth below we set our course for Amman, the capital city of Jordan. To the right were the dazzling snows covering the slopes of Mount Hermon. Beneath us stretched the land dear to us as our own native hills and plains, and possibly in some respects even better known. As far as eye could see were the valleys and the uplands where prophets and apostles and the Saviour Himself had lived and laboured, where generation after generation of the authentic people of God had raised their altars, slain their sacrificial victims, built their temples, and alas, slain also in blind fury the spokesmen of the Lord. Here the Assyrian had come down 'like the wolf on the fold, with cohorts all gleaming in purple and gold'. Here the king, prophetically characterized as 'that head of gold' had destroyed the house 'exceeding magnifical'. Here were the dens and caves where, in evil times, the choicest of men and the very salt of the earth, clad in sheepskins and goat-skins, had taken refuge from the oppressor. Here – wonder of wonders! – the Son of God Himself had been 'made flesh and dwelt among us', for us men and for our salvation. The land, holy before His coming, had become a holy of holies by virtue of His presence, for was not He 'the holy one of God'? In the land spread beneath our eyes He had engaged in combat with sin and Satan. Here was located the spot of ground where He had shed the blood of redemption, the sun the meanwhile 'shutting its glories in' and the solid earth heaving with sym-pathetic pain. Here He had lain awhile keeping sabbatic rest. Here He had risen from His rocky tomb in the power of an end-less life. From one of its hills He had ascended to the excellent glory. William Blake, in wild poetic frenzy may have imagined it otherwise, but it was here, in the land bathed in morning light beneath us, that 'the holy Lamb of God' had been seen on pas-tures of pleasantness. These were the unclouded hills on which the 'countenance divine' had shone forth, even literally so on the tremendous occasion when He had climbed the steeps of 'an exceeding high mountain'.

To the south, threading its way like a writhing snake from one sea to another, the Jordan river sparkled. To the east stretched Gilead and its pasturelands. To the west there were the Judaean highlands, and beyond them, scarcely visible in the far distance, was the Mediterranean, 'the inmost sea of all the earth', still as in ancient times carrying on its blue and tide-less deep the shipping of the world.

To catch a sight of the entire land from Dan to Beersheba, and from eastern desert to western sea, seemed truly a matter of wonder. For the moment we felt ourselves as it were on Nebo, viewing the landscape o'er, and, unlike Moses, we had reached our point of vantage without a vestige of grief.

By 4 o'clock – we had lost an hour on the eastward flight and had to adjust our watches accordingly[1] – we were looking down upon the airport of Amman. Orientals, as we were soon to discover, rise early, but few were as yet astir and, for the moment, we had to kick our heels while awaiting developments. Routine checks and examination of passports proved a slow matter. We sat around in a pleasant hall, obtained Jordan's currency in exchange for sterling [Jordan is in the sterling area] and awaited the cars which were to convey us the same morning to Jerusalem and to our hotel.

Eager to make contact with both land and people, we now found ourselves more than 2,000 miles from home, treading the soil of a land hoary with age when Britain was still the 'ultima Thule' of the geographers, a territory of few people, wild and on the utmost confines of the world. Another sun now shone upon us. Here was warmth in exchange for chill; 'drouth' instead of mist and rain; brightness in place of clouded skies. Here in fact was the Middle East. 'Our pilgrimage', as our tourist agency termed it, was well under way.

*

In my mind I could not help but contrast the ease and speed of our arrival with the discomforts and troubles encountered by

---

[1] The difference between Greenwich Mean Time and Time in the Holy Land is two hours, but British Summer Time accounts for the second hour.

those who went to the Holy Land with tantalizing slowness in the times of the Medieval Crusades. Ships were small and must have been painfully overcrowded, so that those who sailed in them frequently fell a-quarrelling. In consequence Richard I, the English crusading monarch, made certain laws, the following among them:

'Whoever slays a man on shipboard shall be bound to the dead man and thrown into the sea; if on land, he shall be bound to the dead man and buried in the earth.

If a man draws a knife to strike another he shall lose his hand.

A robber convicted of theft shall be shorn, and boiling tar poured on his head, and feathers from a cushion shall be shaken out over his head. At the first land where the ships shall put in he shall be cast on shore'.

I bear witness that the company with which we travelled knew nothing of disputes or quarrels; all was as peaceful as we could wish.

One thing more! Around midnight, as my wife and I sat, perhaps somewhat dreamily, in our corridor seats, one behind the other, a member of the crew at that hour released from duty, entered into conversation by his own desire on the most momentous of all subjects – God, Christ, the Word of God, and the interests and perplexities of the human soul. He professed to be an atheist and had read widely, and, one would judge, thought deeply. Various religions had received his attention. Well educated and well versed in atheistical literature he had seen something of the emptiness and vanity of much that goes by the name of religious profession. He had made contact with sacerdotalism and its gaudy trappings, and his soul had revolted against it. There was an earnestness about his way of thought and manner of speech which we found attractive, and as something of the Gospel of Christ and the integrity of the Word of God was pressed upon his attention, we were moved to pray that the veil upon his eyes might be lifted, and that the great issues of life and death and eternity might be set before him by the Spirit of God Himself.

Conversation with an atheist drives one of necessity to the throne of grace with the plea that the impenetrability of the darkened and stubborn heart might yield to the power of Him who is stronger than the strong. It was as Saul of Tarsus approached Damascus from Jerusalem that scales of unbelief fell from his eyes [were the literal scales that later fell from them in the house of Judas, in the street called Straight, tokens of this?]. Wonderful would it be if similar scales fell from blinded eyes as we flew towards the same city at 350 miles per hour early on a May morning in the year of grace 1967!

THE HOLY LAND

Over the Promised Land, to God so dear;
By which, to visit oft those happy tribes,
On high behests His angels to and fro
Passed frequent, and His eye with choice regard
From Paneas, the fount of Jordan's flood,
To Beersheba, where the Holy Land
Borders on Egypt and the Arabian shore.

JOHN MILTON Paradise Lost iii. 531–537

Here stranger-lives the Patriarchs led,
Here promised Canaan smiled;
From Northern Lebanon outspread
To Araby the wild.

A land of fountains and of rills,
With milk and honey fraught,
Whose stones were iron, from whose hills
Marble and brass were wrought.

A land of corn and wine and oil,
Whose trees with fruitage hung;
While birds to soothe the labourer's toil
Among the branches sung.

Valleys stood thick with golden grain,
Goats bounded on the rocks,
And white and dark, on slope and plain,
Roamed pasturing herds and flocks.

JAMES MONTGOMERY

2

From Amman to Jerusalem

I‍T can be assumed with safety that something of the long and chequered history of Israel is known to all. The Bible itself, considered from one angle, is a history book, carrying the story down to the first century AD. Prophetically it carries it much further [indeed to the times of the end] for prophecy is but the womb of the future, history written in advance of the event.

The twentieth century has seen remarkable happenings. Israel has at long last been restored to part of its own ancient heritage, and to the status of nationhood, and with that restoration Britain has been more intimately associated than has any other nation. The Balfour Declaration of 1917, the Palestine Mandate given to Britain by the League of Nations, the re-settlement of the Jews in the land under the notorious quota system, the establishment of an Independent Jewish State in 1948 – in all of these our compatriots have played a prominent and a major part.

The story of the State of Jordan is, however, not so well known. Jordan, originally called Transjordan, is one of the

States formed after the break-up of the old Turkish Empire as a result of the First World War. Under Turkish rule it had belonged to the vilayet of Damascus. The Mandate for Palestine, given to Britain by the Supreme Council of Allied Powers in conference at San Remo [Italy] in 1920, and confirmed to it by the League of Nations in 1924, included control of Transjordan. The French Government, which had received a Mandate for Syria, agreed that Palestine did not come under that Mandate, but that it fell to Britain.

Britain prepared the land for self-government and in 1946 she recognized it as an independent State in alliance with herself. Abdullah, its king, was assassinated in Jerusalem in 1951, and a year later his grandson, Hussein, became king. Naturally, the creation of the State of Israel, which involved loss of territory by Transjordan and the partition of Jerusalem, was bitterly resented by the Arab State, and relations between the two have always been bad. The name Transjordan was at first used because its territory was chiefly east of the Jordan river, but the incoming of the Jew led to stress upon its claim to the whole of Palestine, and not simply to the land 'across' the river. The claim has never been dropped, and ordnance maps issued by the Jordan government still show the whole of Palestine as coming under King Hussein's sovereignty. The area occupied by Israel is designated 'Occupied Territory' [i.e. occupied by an enemy]. The population of Jordan is a little over two millions, of which about 12% professes the Christian faith. The mass of the population is Moslem. King Hussein reigns as a constitutional monarch with an administration conducted from Amman.

We caught but a fleeting glimpse of Amman, the capital city of the State of Jordan, and formerly the chief city of the Ammonites, the descendants of Lot, Abraham's nephew

[*Genesis* 19.38]. By road it lies about 60 miles from Jerusalem, though it is rather less as the crow flies. It did not lack attractiveness, but we lacked opportunity to walk its streets and look at its citizens and its activities. We were to be taken to Jerusalem almost at once. Jerusalem had its own landing strips, but to accommodate jet planes the strips required to be lengthened, and while this work was being accomplished, planes were diverted to Amman by arrangement with the Jordan government.

We had reached Amman airport about 4 a.m. By 6 there was great activity; we were to journey to Jerusalem [the Jordan part of that city] in cars which carried five or six passengers apiece. Thirty-seater coaches which, in our opinion, would have been [as in Israel] more suited to our need, did not seem to have 'taken' in Jordan. The cars were limousines of American origin, which were comfortable enough, but they were lacking in elevation, and therefore not so advantageous as coaches for the purpose of viewing the Promised Land. The difference of elevation between a car and a coach is that between shanks's mare and a high horse; the coach and the horse extend the traveller's horizon, especially when he is passing through level tracts of country.

The portrait in colour of Jordan's King Hussein is found in all buildings, public if not private. Maybe the fact that he has married an English wife moves his people to regard the English tourist with the greater favour, but as we shortly discovered that the tourist industry is the means of introducing much needed capital into the country, we were not surprised to receive all possible facilities and a warm welcome. We quickly learned also that the King is the active and not merely the titular head of his government, combining, as he appears to do, the kingly office with the work of a prime minister. Before we left

Jordan we were invited to attend in our hotel a showing of coloured slides of the land and its principal places of interest, together with a taped running commentary. It was prefaced by words of welcome to tourists spoken by King Hussein in person, and concluded with views of the king, his wife and his children, and with further words wishing us all happiness and prosperity during our stay in his Hashimite Kingdom. The king claims descent from Hashim, an uncle of Mohammed; 'Hashimite' therefore proclaims the dual nature of the kingdom. It is at once Arab and Moslem.

It so happened that our arrival in Amman coincided with the commencement of a visit being paid by His Majesty to a neighbouring State, and as he walked to his plane on the airfield an English cheer from our company gave thanks by anticipation for the greetings we were later to receive by tape.

At first blush Amman seemed to have little direct connection with the Holy Land proper, and memories of Jephthah reminded us that in his day the territories of the Ammonites and of Israel were most certainly distinct [*Judges* 11]. But Rabbah, or 'Rabbath of the children of Ammon' [*Deuteronomy* 3.11] receives pointed mention in the Old Testament. In 2 *Samuel* 12.27 it is called 'the city of waters', probably because it lies near the sources of the Jabbok [now called the Gerka], a tributary of the Jordan famous in Bible story as the scene of the wrestling of Jacob with the angel [*Genesis* 32.22]. It was while the army of Israel under the command of Joab was fighting for the possession of Rabbath that David fell so foully into sin and attempted to shield himself from public scandal by contriving the murder of Uriah the Hittite, slain by the Ammonites but, as in the sight of the all-seeing Lord God, murdered by royal hands. Hence the later agonizing prayer, 'Deliver me from blood guiltiness, thou God of my salvation' [*Ps.* 51.14]. Sad link with Hebrew history and with the soul pilgrimage of an erring child of God! To what depths can a man of God fall when he lies in luxurious ease and gives liberty to the baser passions!

At a much later date it is recorded [though not in the pages of Scripture] that one of the Egyptian Ptolemies rebuilt Rabbath and added Philadelphia to its name. Later still, in New Testament times, it was one of the cities belonging to Decapolis [*Matt.* 4.25 etc.] and an important centre for trade; several trade routes converged upon it.

But perhaps the most interesting point of all is the incidental mention in *Deuteronomy* 3.11 that at Rabbah was to be seen the bedstead of iron owned by Og, King of Bashan, the territory north of Rabbah. Modern writers interpret this to mean Og's sarcophagus rather than any contraption to hold his giant frame o'nights. They are probably correct. On the other hand it is curious to note that, when David fled from Absalom and took refuge beyond the River Jordan, among those who brought beds for the king's refugee company was Shobi of 'Rabbah of the children of Ammon' [2 *Sam.* 17.27]. May we take it that, for some unknown reason, beds play a significant part in Rabbah's long story?

*

Arab motor-cars are driven at speed even in cities. We never felt that a speed limit applied in any place, though how the law of the land bears on the matter I do not know. The horn is all-important. Its strident note echoes loud in every thoroughfare, and seems to bear a close resemblance to the Arab male voice: and it not only echoes loud, it echoes long. We were given but a short-lived sight of Amman for we saw it while moving at 40 m.p.h. It was the first eastern city on which we set eyes. Here we saw the typical oriental shop with its open access [closed at night by a down-to-the-ground shutter] and with its proprietor normally sitting at the entrance to his premises. It impressed us by the length of its main street – it ran along a fairly narrow winding valley – and by its considerable size. Whereas I had held the vague conception of a city of perhaps 20,000 or 30,000, I discovered to my surprise that it now held almost a quarter of a million inhabitants, and the character of the surrounding country brought wonderment as to how they managed to make a living.

The grounds of the city's 'working palace' and its 'guest palace' are patrolled by colourful Circassian guards wearing black and red robes and high black Cossack hats flying red ribbons. It seemed strange to find men of Circassia [located in the Caucasus Mountains] in the Middle East. Their forefathers had been driven from their native land after the Russo-Turkish war in the late nineteenth century, and the Sultan of Turkey had settled some of them at Amman, which was then a part of his dominions. By their industry they became well-established there.

The hill sides of Amman for a considerable distance are lined with the usual type of flat-topped eastern house, all of stone, interspersed with white limestone villas of a more modern design. We caught sight of the remains of a Roman amphi-theatre built in the 2nd or 3rd century AD. It has three tiers built into the curvature of a hill and accommodated no less than 6,000 spectators. For almost two millenniums it has borne eloquent testimony to 'the grandeur that was Rome'.

The road we travelled was remarkably good, as in fact were almost all of the motor ways which we used in Jordan, and at times our enthusiastic Jehu touched 80 m.p.h. He enjoyed speed more than did his passengers. But even in the city of

Amman the side walks were normally little better than earthen paths, uneven and dusty to the feet. On the outskirts of the capital a sheep market was in progress. We should like to have paused to listen to the harangue and the bargaining, and to have read the pros and cons of the affair in the faces of the crowd, but our chariot would not stay.

Limestone hills in various shades of grey and brown showed an occasional splash of green, but there was little sign of cultivation and we could form little idea of the source from which sheep and goat and camel obtained sustenance. Shortly, for mile after mile, we saw nothing but hills barren from base to summit, and as empty of tree and shrub, and even tufts of grass of any description, as the sky was empty of clouds. Bedouin shanties, black, ugly and tattered in appearance – and yet home to the hillside Arab – could be seen perched in anything but splendid isolation on the arid stony slopes, but after a while even these ceased to be, and the terrain became as bleak and uninviting as the mountains of the moon. Until the Jordan valley came in sight, the entire landscape seemed utterly desolate, parched and barren. Not a green blade was to be seen in a territory once reputed to yield rich harvests. 'A fruitful land [turned] into barrenness' – the Psalmist's description of a fertile field which has become a wilderness – was the sentence writ large over the landscape.

Bedouin tents are always black, like the tents of Kedar [*Song of Sol.* 1.5]. They could hardly be otherwise, for black goats' hair woven into the cloth to give it greater durability is used in their construction. Quite possibly the cloth made by the tentmakers of Cilicia, of whom Saul of Tarsus was one, found its way southwards to this area. Who knows! Tents as made by the Bedouins appear to change nothing of their pattern from one century, or even one millennium, to another.

They symbolize the unchanging East. They are rectangular structures, made from cloth thrown over a framework of poles. That is all. One of the longer sides of the rectangle is always left open. Pegs, such as that driven by Jael through the temples of Sisera, nail the structure to the ground. The central ridge of the tent is as high as a tall man [Arabs usually possess height!] and from it the back and sides slope to the ground. Beds are made on the ground, sometimes on the bare earth itself, bone dry as it is, but normally they are raised a little from the ground if sticks or reeds are available. Elaborate bed-clothes are the less necessary because the only difference between dress by day and that by night is that the girdle is removed during rest. As soon as he rises, the Bedouin fastens the girdle around his long white outer robe. The process of dressing thus takes but a moment, that of washing even less, for the scarcity of water at most times of the year tends to render ablutions an infrequent luxury.

*

Forty miles or so from Amman we came within sight of the Dead Sea and the Jordan valley. No longer could the area be described as like 'the garden of the Lord' [*Gen.* 13.10]; desert conditions were still painfully evident, but it was a relief to descend into the Jordan trough and certainly a joy to have this first sight of 'The Descender', for such seems to be a possible meaning of the name of the river familiar to the ears of every Christian and one of the subjects of his songs. I made the discovery that the 'rift valley' of the Jordan was much wider at this particular point than my imaginings had led me to expect. Certainly the Jordan itself was no wider or deeper than a small English river, but the valley as a whole possessed a breadth which I found impressive, and which helped me to understand the better how Joshua and the vast host that followed him [vast as shown by the two recorded censuses after the departure from Egypt] could find room to encamp before the 'devoted city' which was the first object of their attack.

Some distance beyond the spot where stands the notice SEA LEVEL by the roadside we reached the Allenby bridge over the Jordan and were informed that we were near the spot where the Lord Jesus Christ was baptized. We could well believe it. No doubt many of the traditional sites of the Holy Land are little more than conjectural, but some bear the clear marks of reality much more than do others. In this case it was easy to imagine 'all the land of Judaea and they of Jerusalem' making their dusty way to this particular place. Here then, so far as can be known, the Lord from heaven humbled Himself in baptism for our sakes, fulfilling all righteousness, and despite the Baptist's objections, insisting on immersion beneath the muddy waters. Here above Him, as He came up out of the water, the heavens opened, and the Spirit descended upon Him in bodily shape like a dove, while the Father testified, 'Thou art my beloved Son; in Thee I am well pleased'. Thus was witness borne to His Messiahship and Sonship. Here, or at some distance upstream, the Baptist announced Him as the Lamb of God, and here, as He walked, the question was addressed to Him by the first disciples, 'Master, where dwellest Thou?'. Discipleship was born at the Jordan.

It would have been high privilege to tread the hallowed ground but our driver passed at speed and in a few minutes we were ascending the famous road which threads its way between the hills, still barren, separating the city of the curse from the city of God. The sign SEA LEVEL greeted us on this side the river as its twin sign had done on the eastern side. Shortly we found ourselves passing through Bethany on its pleasant hill, and mounting the slopes of Olivet. Then, in a few moments, rounding a bend in the road, we had our first sight of Jerusalem.

There was no need for us to veil our eyes, as Lion Heart is reported to have done when, having reached Emmaus on the opposite side of the holy city, he refused to look upon a place which he lacked strength to conquer, and resolutely held his shield before his face. To us the sight was superb. The day was yet young. We have lost count of time, but it must have been about 9 o'clock. Morning light illuminated valley and hill, the walls, and the historic splendours of the city. Viewed from a distance it seemed, like the 'daughter' of Psalm 45, 'all glorious within', its clothing of wrought gold. As Wordsworth's London,

> *'This city now doth like a garment wear*
> *The beauty of the morning. . . .*
> *Never did sun more beautifully steep*
> *In his first splendour valley, rock, or hill.'*

'Bright and glittering' as London might be 'in the smokeless air', Jerusalem seemed much more so. There was advantage in looking not merely upon it, but down upon it, for the fact that 'the mountains are round about Jerusalem', including some of superior height, requires one so to do. It was much as I had imagined it to be from photographs and drawings which I had seen, but again, its amplitude took me by surprise. I had under-estimated its dimensions, but could now enter into the meaning of words written by an American Samuel Johnson [who, as it happens, was born in *Salem*, Massachusetts],

> *'City of God, how broad and far*
> *Outspread thy walls sublime'*.

I saw it and marvelled. At the same time I realized the force of the Psalmist's reference to the kings who had 'assembled and passed by together' without daring to attack it [*Ps.* 48.4]. 'Fear took hold upon them there, and pain, as of a woman in travail; they were troubled and hasted away'. In a sense impossible to them, we were able to claim the city as our own, 'the city of our God', vivid type of

> *'Jerusalem, my happy home,*
> *Name ever dear to me!'*

As we had heard, so now had we seen. Shortly we were to look upon some of the abominations within the place, and to note the signs of the refusal of the name and authority of the 'Great King' whose city it was and is. But for the moment the superficial tinsel glory prevailed:

> *'How rise thy towers, serene and bright,*
> *To meet the dawning day.'*

It was about a week later, after we had passed through the Mandelbaum Gate and were touring the Israeli part of the city, that the leader of our party read to us the delightful and appropriate words found in the psalm just quoted:

> *'Beautiful for situation, the joy of the whole earth is Mount Zion, on the sides of the north, the city of the great King ... Walk about Zion, and go round about her: tell the towers thereof. Mark ye well her bulwarks, consider her palaces, that ye may tell it to the generation following';*
>
> [PSALM 48]

or to give them in the Scottish metrical version:

> *'Mount Zion stands most beautiful,*
> *the joy of all the land;*
> *The city of the mighty King*
> *on her north side doth stand.*

[35]

Walk about Zion, and go round;
the high tow'rs thereof tell:
Consider ye her palaces,
and mark her bulwarks well;

That ye may tell posterity.
for this God doth abide
Our God for evermore; He will
ev'n unto death us guide.'

Often had we read the words, 'Our feet shall stand within thy gates, O Jerusalem'. And now an experience which hitherto we had never in our wildest dreams supposed to be within the bounds of rational possibility had become ours. Looking on 'the mountain of God's holiness', we were on the threshold of 'the city of the great King', once 'the holy place of the tabernacles of the Most High'. High privilege indeed!

The sight will ever abide in the memory. In coming days I expect it to 'flash upon that inward eye which is the bliss of solitude', and when that happens the heart will thrill again with the pleasure of it. I almost felt, as we 'gazed and gazed' [as did the poet on a very different scene], that we had acquired a new form of wealth.

From another point of view, it was as though time had assumed a new dimension. Within the space of twelve hours after leaving Gatwick Airport in Surrey, we had taken our leave of England, crossed Europe from the English Channel to the Adriatic, flown over half the length of the Mediterranean, penetrated Asia, seen the river which for two thousand years has symbolized the frontier between this present world and the world to come, and obtained a glorious sight of earth's first city, type of the 'city of the living God' Himself, 'the heavenly Jerusalem', the city which will one day be seen 'coming down from God out of heaven, prepared as a bride adorned for her husband'. 'See Naples and die' runs an adage well known in past days. For 'Naples' substitute 'Mount Zion', and for the moment let your 'bounding heart forget to beat'.

JERUSALEM

The air sublime,
Over the wilderness, and o'er the plain,
Till underneath them fair Jerusalem,
The Holy City, lifted high her towers;
And higher yet the glorious temple reared
Her pile, far off appearing like a mount
Of alabaster – topt with golden spires.

JOHN MILTON Paradise Regained iv. 542–548

3

'*Jerusalem*
...
Jerusalem'

Arrived in Jerusalem, we found the situation and service of our hotel very agreeable. Accommodation in the heart of the city would have been convenient, but to live for a week on the lower slopes of the Mount of Olives, and to find it necessary to enter the city by crossing the brook Kidron [Cedron] appealed even more to our hearts. Not that the brook was actually there! Its watercourse was dry, though I surmise that in the rainy season it might be found occasionally flowing with water. There was evidence of this in a lower part of the Valley, where the natural bed of the stream had given place to a concrete conduit, which suggested that from time to time the brook could boast an existence. I crossed the dry bed daily, and could readily enter into the simple beauty of the words in John's Gospel, 'When Jesus had spoken these words, He went forth with His disciples over the brook Cedron' [18.1]. In a different fashion David had done so when he fled from Absalom his son, and set his face 'toward the way of the wilderness' [2 *Sam.* 15.23] that is to say, towards the east bank of the Jordan. Perchance along the very road on the side of which our hotel was located,

[41]

and by which we had first seen the city, 'he went up by the ascent of Mount Olivet, and wept as he went up, and had his head covered, and he went barefoot: and all the people that was with him covered every man his head, and they went up, weeping as they went up' [2 *Sam.* 15.30].

Despite the up-to-dateness of transport [bus and limousine], and the ever-present sounding of the car horns, the Old Testament was very much alive to us as we moved in and out of the city. It was as if antiquity and modernity were yoked together in incongruous fellowship. Most mornings I paused awhile to watch a baggy-trousered Arab, very obviously one of the poor of the land, ploughing a field alongside the Kidron. His sorry little beast – whether mule or ass or horse I could not make up my mind – drew what I must call a plough. It looked from a short distance like a mere pointed stick, though possibly it was of metal [it seemed to possess the rough shape of a diamond], and I could well believe that it could claim close kinship with instruments used by the Canaanites four or five thousand years ago. A traveller of 130 years ago described a similar plough as 'made entirely of wood, the coulter only being sheathed in a very thin plate of iron, exceedingly light, and fit to be guided by a single hand.' He added, 'We at once saw how easy a matter it would be literally to beat their swords into ploughshares'. It was almost unbelievable that, under the walls of a world-renowned city, agriculture should have remained static while Persians, Greeks, Romans, Crusaders, Turks and others had come and gone. Another mark of the 'unchanging East'! It was almost as much a surprise to me as was the fishing up of a coelacanth in the Indian Ocean to scientists in 1938, the breed which zoological experts who held evolutionary theories had spoken of as 'extinct sixty million years ago'.

Another simple sight below the walls of Jerusalem gave me

almost equal pleasure. It reminded me of the fact that, in the gardens [and I may almost say woods] of South Kensington, it is possible to sit, as if in the heart of the country, and watch sheep grazing, the sole reminder of the true locality being 'London's central roar' as it breaks the silence. Here, under the shadow of Jerusalem's walls, were small flocks of sheep and goats attended by their shepherds. There seemed to be no necessity for the shepherds to 'make them to rest at noon' [*Song of Sol.* 1.7]; the shade of a large olive tree brought them closely together in mid-day repose. As for the long-haired goats, some of them by rearing themselves on their hind legs seemed capable of cropping the olives some seven or eight feet from the ground. Somehow, they did not seem to rest as did the sheep. There were no fields or fences after the English fashion.

*

On our first morning, while some of the members of our party rested in the hotel after the sleeplessness of the night, I already felt the refreshment and invigoration of the Jerusalem air, and was anxious to make acquaintance with the city itself. The first building to attract my attention as I entered was Jordan's Museum of Antiquities. Its collections were impressive and I was glad to find a section devoted to the Dead Sea scrolls. When the Exhibition of the Scrolls visited various parts of Britain I missed it, but was now able to make good the deficiency. The principal finds in the Cwmran caves did not seem to be on view [maybe they are held by Israel], but there were to be seen scrolls which included fragments of Genesis, Exodus, Leviticus [in the Septuagint version], Jeremiah, and the Lamentations. It seemed that the most popular parts of the Old Testament, if one may form a judgment based on the comparative numbers of scrolls discovered, were Deuteronomy,

the Psalms, Isaiah, and the Minor Prophets. A substantial
number of the finds on the site of ancient Jericho were also on
view.

In the afternoon of this first day we made our first planned
excursion – to the Church of the Ascension on the upper slopes
of the Mount of Olives. It is beyond question that the ascension
took place from Olivet, but one cannot help but feel that the
traditional site is not near enough to Bethany to fulfil the requirements of *Luke* 24.50: 'He led them out as far as to Bethany'. Be this as it may, where ecclesiastical buildings are erected
over sacred spots, verisimilitude promptly takes its flight.
Hence the insistence in these pages on what is natural rather than
upon the artificial. The natural setting, so far as it can be determined, promotes spiritual appreciation, whereas the fine
buildings erected by man detract from it, and despite the
beauty of architecture, prove in some cases quite obnoxious.

In the Church of the Ascension is shown an impression of
Christ's right foot, turned southwards. A guide book of fame
explains that for a long time 'the footprint has been so variously
described that it must have been frequently renewed'. We could
well believe it. In the New Testament no mention is made as to
the actual place of the second advent, though the impression is
certainly conveyed that it will be at, or in the near neighbourhood of Jerusalem; but from *Zech.* 14.4, which it is impossible
to regard as having been fulfilled, it may well be concluded that
the Lord's return will be to the very spot from which He left
the earth:

> *'And when Thou comest for Thy saints,*
> *'Twill be at Bethany.'*

Again, at leisure, we viewed the striking panorama of the
holy city. Beneath our eyes stretched walls, churches, mosques,

minarets, towers, and other buildings without number, some of which we were to inspect in detail before we left for Galilee. The genuine relics of Bible days were what we wished chiefly to see. As for the rest, historians and churches could be left to quarrel over them. Disputes about keys and stars, though they contributed to the outbreak of the Crimean War of the eighteen-fifties, were not within our orbit of interest. We were to visit 'ecclesiastical' spots as belonging to the 'sights' of the Holy Land, and would behave with due circumspection, but without becoming enamoured of them.

Thus it was, for instance, at the Church of the HolySepulchre. Its history, dating from the time of the Emperor Constantine and Helena his mother in the fourth century, is given in the principal guide books, in some of them in great detail. In *this* particular spot, for example, the Lord is said to have appeared to Mary Magdalene [*John* 20.14–15]; in *that*, is said to stand the stone of unction where Nicodemus wrapped his myrrh and aloes inside the linen bands of sepulture. But the entire place and atmosphere are so unrealistic that I and others almost felt disinclined to make the circuit of the building, and when we found that there was a long queue waiting to enter the tiny Chapel of the Holy Sepulchre where candles supplied a dim religious light and where stones were kissed, we gladly made our exit from the building. I declined a sprinkling with holy water which one of the priests in attendance invited me to undergo.

Meanwhile we became separated from our party, but were aware of their unseen presence as the notes of 'When I survey the wondrous cross' reached our ears from afar. 'Long-drawn aisle', 'fretted vault', and 'pealing anthem' may cater for the aesthetic taste, whether in the homeland or elsewhere, but so far as their eastern counterparts are intended to render commemorative the 'holy places' of Palestine, the effect is inimical to spirituality.

Personally I have long had an interest in matters archaeological, not least in connection with Jerusalem as the city where God 'placed His Name', and at this point I include a short account of the city's topography and significance which I wrote some time ago for the *Bible League Quarterly*. It covers Old Testament times only, but includes material basic to an understanding of Jerusalem's long and tragic story.

*

Considerable difficulties have existed for those who have endeavoured to solve the topographical problems which Jerusalem presents. Probably more frequently than any other city, Jerusalem has been captured and destroyed. It has been termed the '27-times-destroyed city'. Yet upon the ruins of the old city a new city has invariably arisen. Jerusalem has proved indestructible. 'In many places', writes an archaeologist, 'the debris that conceals the old city from our sight is over a hundred feet deep. Laborious and expensive excavations are therefore everywhere necessary in order to arrive at any degree of certitude regarding the form of the ancient city. In many places these are impossible, inasmuch as upon the debris the new houses of the modern city have been built, underneath which digging cannot be done'. Jerusalem's very indestructibility has been in itself the greatest of hindrances to the archaeologist. Whereas Babylon and Nineveh, for example, are desolate ruins, where 'diggers up of the past' have had free scope, Jerusalem has risen phoenix-like from its ashes and the excavator is correspondingly handicapped. And outside the bounds of the modern city, as in the valley of the Kidron and the Valley of Hinnom, the presence of thousands of graves both Jewish and

Moslem, renders the task of the archaeologist one of great difficulty. In the temple area, again, investigation is all but forbidden upon religious grounds. Yet of recent years experts have been able to reach reliable conclusions on certain matters which have been long in dispute.

Apart from the important fact that it is situated near the point where three continents meet, Jerusalem's vast importance in human history owes little, if anything, to its geographical situation. It is not on the sea-coast, nor is it easy of access from the sea, for the roads from the Mediterranean wind through steep and rugged mountain valleys. Unlike many great capitals, ancient and modern, it is not situated on a river. Nor has it been a mart of nations, situated where trade-routes converge. It lies in fact on no great highway. The surrounding country is not remarkable for any special degree of fertility; on the contrary, it is somewhat more arid and less productive than some other parts of the Holy Land. Its importance is due to the fact that God chose to 'place His Name there': hence it has established itself in the affections of the Jewish people and in the interest of Christians as has no other city on the face of the earth.

The traveller goes up to Jerusalem. If he journeys there from the shores of the Mediterranean he climbs 2500 feet above sea level. If he makes the ascent from Jericho and the Dead Sea he rises 3800 feet. Palestine has a backbone of mountains which form the watershed between the Mediterranean and the Jordan Valley, and on the summit of this ridge Jerusalem stands. It is surrounded, however, by hills of slightly greater height, so that no extensive prospect is to be met with, except to the south-east where there is a gap in the outer ring, and the mountains of Moab, at the western edge of the great Arabian desert, are to be seen 25 to 30 miles away.

*

Geologically considered, Jerusalem rests on the chalky lime-stone of the Judean hills. Beds of limestone having a gentle south-easterly slope are found immediately below the city. The lower strata reach ground level on the city's western ridge, and consist of a hard stone suitable for building and for paving stones. Above these are beds of softer fine white limestone, known as 'royal stone'. This has been used extensively for building purposes. Underneath the city ancient quarries exist which probably supplied all the stones needed for the construction of Solomon's temple. On this softer rock rest more beds of hard grey limestone, which appear on the slopes of the Mount of Olives to the east of Jerusalem. The rocks of the district contain no metals, and such clay as occurs is of rather poor quality. Much of Jerusalem's limestone is porous. The rain sinks through it to considerable depths and is deflected by harder underlying rocks towards the south-east of the city where are found the only well and spring in the near neighbourhood.

On three sides Jerusalem is surrounded by deep-cut ravines. In ancient times they were much deeper than they are today. Great accumulations of debris, resulting from the oft-repeated deliberate and systematic destruction of the city, have reduced the depth by 50 or 60 feet in some places, with the consequence that the modern visitor often fails to appreciate the military advantages of the site in ancient days. Those who study the site from photographs are also easily deceived. Modern science has completely altered conceptions of military strategy, but in old times Jerusalem was regarded as occupying a well-nigh im-pregnable position. It was the Gibraltar of the Palestinian high-lands. *Lamentations* 4.12 shows the sense of surprise which affected the kings and peoples of the earth 'who would not have believed that the adversary and the enemy should have entered into the gates of Jerusalem'. Joshua failed to capture the city [then called Jebus], and David, before he took it, had to meet the taunts and jeers of its inhabitants who mocked him with the news that the citadel could well be defended by the blind and the lame.

On the east of the city runs the aforementioned Kidron valley, separating it from the Mount of Olives. Further north it separates the city from Mount Scopus upon which the Roman Emperor Titus and his legions encamped during the siege of Jerusalem in AD 70. It deepens rapidly towards its southern end and becomes a narrow ravine with 'tolerably precipitous sides'. When it leaves the outskirts of Jerusalem it runs on towards the Dead Sea and becomes increasingly rugged.

To the west of Jerusalem runs the valley anciently called the Valley of Hinnom or of the Sons of Hinnom. It turns abruptly eastward as soon as it has passed the city's western ridge, deepens rapidly, and joins the Kidron at the so-called Well of Job [Bir Eyyub] at the city's south-east corner. It was in this Valley that Manasseh practised the worship of Moloch and 'caused his children to pass through the fire', for which reason the godly Josiah, his grandson, defiled it, making it a receptable for the bodies of criminals. A fire was kept perpetually burning there, and worms were continually gendering in the putrifying flesh. The valley thus became a vivid image of hell, the destined place for all unfit for the city of God. The term 'Gehenna', as used in the New Testament and translated 'hell', is really a Greek form of the name 'Ge-Hinnom' [Valley of Hinnom]. Tophet was a spot in this valley [2 Kings 23.10]. It is referred to several times by Jeremiah, and was apparently the centre of idolatrous worship, on which account it came to be regarded as a fit symbol of the place 'ordained of old' [Isa. 30.33] for the punishment of the ungodly.

Aceldama, 'the field of blood' [Matt. 27.6–8] was situated in the same locality. It so happened that the area also contained a pocket of clay suitable for the use of potters. Probably the clay was so far exhausted by the time of Christ's betrayal that the field where it had been worked was of no further value for the potters. It could therefore be applied to a different use, while it retained the name of 'the potter's field'. Then, too, the Valley of Hinnom was the boundary fixed in the days of Joshua between the tribes of Judah and Benjamin [*Josh.* 15.8 and 18.16]. The temple hill, therefore, was actually situated within the territory of Benjamin, which lay to the north of the valley.

Between the Kidron and Hinnom valleys occurs a third valley, probably as deeply cut in the rock as the others, but so completely filled in with the debris of centuries that it has lost much of its ancient character and is now a comparatively slight trough dividing the hills which form its flanks. It runs from north to south, thus dividing the ancient city into eastern and western portions. It is not mentioned in the Bible, but Josephus calls it the Tyropoeon, or the Valley of the Cheesemongers. It was once between twenty and thirty feet deeper than it is today.

Thus Jerusalem is situated on a chalky plateau, an infertile tongue of land of about 900 acres in extent. The northern side is the only side not cut off by ravines from the surrounding country. Andrew Bonar, in his *Palestine for the Young*, compares the valleys to 'fosses scooped out by the Creator' – he does not say 'by Nature' – 'to make Jerusalem secure as a fortress: while on the north side the ground was in a great measure level, that the city might be approached as by a natural drawbridge'.

The high ground in the south-east of Jerusalem and overlooking the Kidron Valley is of peculiar interest because it is undoubtedly the site of the Jebusite city captured by David, which henceforth was called 'the city of David'. Professor G. A. Smith suggested for it the name 'Davidsburgh'. It was anciently known as Ophel, and is important in the unfolding of the city's story.

*

At this point reference must be made to the all-important matter of Jerusalem's water supply, for the location of springs of water helped to determine the earlier history of the city. Modern Jerusalem obtains most of its water from rock-cisterns, with which it is well-supplied, and from aqueducts which introduce water from without. It possesses only two natural sources of supply in its own neighbourhood, and these, strikingly enough, are the only two mentioned in the Bible. They are both situated in the place where the geological factors already outlined would lead us to expect them, namely, at the confluence of the three principal valleys and at or near their lowest point. Here the water which has percolated through the limestone of the plateau finds a vent. There is no doubt that the spring and well of today, which are known respectively as the Virgin's Fountain [or The Staircase Well] and Job's Well, correspond with the sources of water supply which the Old Testament calls Gihon and Enrogel. It was at the latter that Adonijah proclaimed himself king when David his father was old and decrepit, and at Gihon that Solomon was proclaimed king on the instruction of David [1 *Kings* 1.9, 33]. *Joshua* 18.16 makes it clear that Enrogel was to be found in or near the valley of Hinnom, and this is sufficient reason for identifying it with the present Job's Well. Gihon is stated in 2 *Chronicles* 33.14 to have been in the Valley of the Kidron, and it could not have any other location than the Virgin's Fountain.

These two sources of water are in the immediate neighbourhood of the eastern ridge. The ridge west of Jerusalem is without a natural water supply. It follows, therefore, that for use as a fortress in ancient times, the eastern ridge would probably be chosen in preference to the western. That such was actually the case is the view of most modern archaeologists, who have forsaken the older belief, dating from the days of Josephus, that the south-west ridge was Zion, the city of David, though a few of them still also hold that both eastern and western hills were included within Jebusite Jerusalem. The south-west hill is about a hundred feet higher than the south-east hill, and to that extent it overlooks it. It is much broader than Ophel and affords much more room for settlement. Using modern weapons, a force occupying the higher hill would have an advantage over a force occupying the lower hill. In ancient warfare, however, this would not be the case. Nor does the smallness of Ophel provide an argument in favour of the older traditional view. Ancient fortresses in Palestine were notoriously small. Gezer, Jericho, and Samaria afford illustrations of this. Exceptions there were, but they are comparatively few. It was customary to mass the houses together within the natural limits of a fortress, and to accept a great congestion of population as a necessary evil, if evil it was held to be. Economy of space was of supreme importance and all other considerations, including sanitation, were regarded as of little concern.

There is very little doubt that Ophel, the south-eastern hill, was the part which David captured from the Jebusites. The identification seems fully to correlate with Old Testament information. It is indeed the problem of the water supply which gives finality to the matter. A completely sterile hill could not endure a siege, and the western hill would not be chosen as a fortress-site for this reason. *The Cambridge Ancient History* pronounces with great assurance on this point: 'The argument from proximity of water, together with the great strength of the Eastern Ridge [within the limitations of ancient warfare], has gradually convinced all but a few, who still cling to the former identification; and it has been powerfully, one might almost venture to say overwhelmingly, reinforced by the most recent excavations.'

These excavations are of outstanding interest and throw valuable light on several Old Testament situations. They show how the inhabitants of the city of David solved the problem of water-supply. Naturally it was only the upper part of the hill which constituted the ancient city. It was, as with many other sites in Palestine, a case of 'a city set on an hill'. Its crags were natural walls of defence ['the munitions of rocks'] and these were rendered still more formidable and unscaleable by a wall, which made it a virtual impossibility for the city to be taken by direct assault. Yet Enrogel and Gihon were in the valley, outside the walls, and it was essential for the inhabitants to have a supply of water which could not be cut off by an enemy. In addition, it was a toilsome matter for the women of the city to descend the very steep slope of the hill in time of peace, and even more so to make the ascent back again with their heavy water jars.

The Jebusites found a very ingenious solution of their difficulty. The archaeologist, R. A. Stewart Macalister, described it thus: 'A tunnel was constructed which may be likened, very roughly, to the letter Z, except that the central member should be vertical and not oblique. The upper horizontal stroke represents a passage that starts from an opening inside the city: the lower, another passage running inwards from the end of the cave in which the water rises. The water-drawers made their way along the upper tunnel, lowered their buckets down the vertical shaft, and so drew up water that flowed into the lower tunnel. We may suppose that the outer entrance of the spring was concealed temporarily or permanently with masonry, thus preventing the access of enemies, who would find no water except perhaps at Bir Eyyub, some distance down the valley'.

*

It is clear from 2 *Samuel* 5 that David experienced unusual difficulty in capturing the hill fort on Ophel. Finally he offered the position of 'chief and captain' of his army to the man who by valour and skill effected the capture. The task involved 'getting up to the gutter' in order that the Jebusites might be smitten. The term used for 'gutter' [sinnor] has presented much difficulty to translators. It appears to mean a watercourse of some kind. In older times it was supposed to mean a gully on the hillside, but now there is little if any doubt that it refers to the rock-hewn passage leading through the hill from Gihon into the heart of the fortress. The work of climbing the vertical portion of the shaft [44 feet high] must have been supremely difficult, if one may judge from the condition of the shaft when rediscovered exactly a century ago by Sir Charles Warren, and named after him. The walls of the shaft were very smooth [this is supposed to indicate that the women of the city used buckets of skins, which polished the rocky sides] and provided no hand-grip or foothold. But the task was accomplished successfully by Joab, who thereby proved his courage and resourcefulness. Macalister writes of his feat thus: 'I myself followed Joab's example when I explored the tunnel; I passed through at dead of night. . . . Wading through the water in the cave, carrying their weapons and probably a rope, they entered the tunnel that opens at the back of the cave. They would follow it west for 32 feet, after which it turns abruptly north and runs for 23 feet by a branch passage, impassable except at low water. Here in Joab's time the tunnel ended in a chamber, at the side of which rose a vertical shaft about 50 feet high. Some expert climber in the party clambered up. . . . With the help of a rope another and then another drew himself up until they were all landed safely in the little chamber at the top of the shaft. From this they passed along the upper passage, which gradually rises by a gentle slope to the flight of steps at the end. Mounting these, they stood within the city'.

It has been conjectured that the Jebusite women left a rope dangling down the shaft and that this provided the solution to Joab's problem. We do not know, but it is all but certain that it was by this perilous enterprise that the Jebusite stronghold fell to David and became his capital city. It has been further supposed that a Jebusite within the city must have assisted David to capture it. Another expert in archaeology [J. Garrow Duncan] has written: 'Unless we suppose that Joab had a confederate inside the city, or that the rope was habitually left dangling in the shaft, I do not think that it was possible for any man to climb this shaft.' It has even been supposed that Araunah, the owner of the threshing floor on Mount Moriah [alongside Ophel], which David bought for the temple-site, was the Jebusite who became confederate with the Hebrews, but there is no proof of this. It is curious, however, that he should be spared after the capture of the city, and that he should be allowed what was obviously a privileged position as a landed proprietor.

There have been other suggestions about the meaning of the word translated 'gutter' in the Authorized Version. Dr W. F. Albright [a leading archaeologist of recent years] has stated that in his view the word probably means 'hook'. He compares it with a similar word used by the Assyrians at a later date for apparatus for scaling walls. Dr Yigael Yadin, Professor of Archaeology in the Hebrew University of Jerusalem, in *The art of warfare in biblical lands in the light of archaeological discovery* [1963], supports a supposition of the late Professor

Sukenik that the Hebrew word '*zinnor*' should not be translated as 'gutter' but as a weapon rather like a three-pronged
pitchfork or trident. 'The Hebrew letter for "and" is "w", and
"w" is also the Hebrew suffix for "his". By moving the letter
"w" back one space in the text and reading it as the suffix of
"zinnor" rather than as a prefix for the succeeding word, we
would get the following phrase which would make the action
clear: "Whosoever . . . smiteth . . . the lame and the blind with
his trident. . . ." '. If this solution is to be adopted, it follows of
course that the supposition that 'zinnor' refers to the underground water-tunnel is no longer tenable.

*

At a later date other devices were arranged for conducting the
waters of Gihon into Jerusalem. At a time unknown, but
probably in the days of the early monarchy, a simple aqueduct
was cut into the side of the hill, and covered over with masonry,
to conduct the overflow of the Gihon spring to a spot at the
south end of Ophel called the old Pool of Siloam, known latterly as Birket-el-Hamra or the Red Pool. It is to this channel
in the hillside that Isaiah appears to refer [8.6] when he speaks
of 'the waters of Shiloah which flow gently'; that is to say, they
lack the rush and tumult of an ordinary stream. Bishop Heber
seemed to have these waters in mind when he wrote of 'cool
Siloam's shady rill'. The word 'Shiloah' means 'Sent' or 'Conducted', and there is reference to this in Christ's words to the
man born blind [*John* 9.7].

Hezekiah was not fully satisfied with arrangements as he
found them. When threatened by the king of Assyria, he gave
careful and doubtless prayerful thought to the question of
Jerusalem's water-supply, and in a skilful way he both denied
water to the Assyrians and conserved it for the use of his own

people ['Why should the kings of Assyria come and find much water?' 2 *Chron.* 32.2–5]. His method was the construction of another tunnel, from Gihon to the southern end of Ophel, to replace the former surface channel. Its value lay in the fact that it was completely hidden from the enemy. The work also included the building-over and concealing of the spring of Gihon. About the same time, apparently, the vertical shaft of the Jebusites was rendered useless. The water was not conducted through the new tunnel to the old pool, but a new pool was made, not far from the first but on somewhat higher ground, inside Ophel. This upper pool is the Pool of Siloam of later Scripture.

Hezekiah's engineers commenced to excavate their tunnel from Gihon and Siloam simultaneously, and successfully accomplished the difficult feat of making both ends meet. We can admire their skill the more when we realize that the tunnel is by no means the shortest distance between the two points. For a reason unknown, but possibly to avoid disturbing the tombs of the kings of Judah, the tunnel winds about. More than once a part of the tunnel forms a short cul-de-sac, indicating that the engineers were not always sure of their way: but they completed their work. The height of the tunnel [which is about a third of a mile in length] varies from 12 feet at the Siloam end to about 6 feet at Gihon. At most intermediate points it is considerably less.

To celebrate the completion of the work, the famous Siloam inscription was engraved. It was discovered about six yards from the Siloam end of the tunnel, and consists of six lines of Hebrew. Professor Sayce, in *'The Higher Criticism and the Monuments'* [1893], writes thus about it:

In the summer [of 1880] some native pupils of Mr Schick, a German architect long settled in Jerusalem, were wading in the Pool of Siloam and the part of the tunnel which opens into it, when one of them slipped and fell into the water. On rising to the surface he noticed what appeared to be letters cut in the rock. . . . Mr Schick visited the spot and at once saw that an ancient inscription had been found. . . . In the winter after the discovery I arrived at Jerusalem, and one of my first visits was to the newly-found inscription. . . . Not only was it difficult to determine the forms of the letters; it was necessary to sit for hours in the mud and water of the channel deciphering them as best one could by the dim light of a candle. It was not until three afternoons had been spent in this fashion that I had the satisfaction of obtaining a text . . . which proved to be a record of the construction of the conduit written in pure biblical Hebrew. The inscription consisted of six lines but a few letters have been destroyed by the wearing away of the stone. The translation of it runs thus:

'[Behold] the excavation! Now this is the history of the excavation. While the excavators were lifting up the pick, each towards his neighbour, and while there were yet three cubits [to excavate, there was heard] the voice of one man calling to his neighbour, for there was an excess in the rock on the right hand [and on the left]. And after that on the day of excavating, the excavators had struck pick against pick, one against the other, the waters flowed from the Spring to the Pool for a distance of 1200 cubits. And a hundred cubits was the height of the rock over the heads of the excavators.'

The inscription is full of linguistic interest, as it proves the identity of the Hebrew spoken in Jerusalem before the Exile with that of our present Old Testament books. At the time when the inscription of Siloam was written the Hebrew language was already that which is embodied in the biblical text.

*

But we must go back in Hebrew history 250 years and make contact with Solomon. In his reign interest is naturally concentrated on the development of the temple hill which lay north of Ophel, and reached to a greater height. This hill is called Moriah in 2 *Chronicles* 3.1, and it is undoubtedly intended to imply that it is the hill on which Abraham offered up his son Isaac, as narrated in *Genesis* 22. The name occurs only in these two places in Scripture. In other words, *Genesis* 22 is divinely intended to be, not only a foreview of the sacrifice of the Son of God Himself, but also an indication of the exact locality where the Messiah should in the fulness of time offer Himself without spot to God.

It is in keeping with this that we are told that Abraham took a three days' journey from Beersheba before reaching the mountain chosen by God for the sacrificial act. The circumstance that the aforementioned Araunah used the temple rock as a threshing floor in the later days of David indicates the eminence of the site. Why Araunah and his sons [four are mentioned in 1 *Chron.* 21.20] were spared when Ophel was captured we can only conjecture. The statement of 2 *Samuel* 24.23 is somewhat puzzling. Many scholars have been loth to believe that Araunah [or Ornan] had been king of Jebus, and have preferred to translate with the Revised Version, 'All this, O King, doth Araunah give unto the King'. But this involves a change both of order and of tense, for the Hebrew clearly reads, 'The whole gave Araunah the king to the king'. Rather than tamper with the text, it is simpler and better to take the statement as it stands and to accept it as one of the unexplained mysteries of the Word.

Solomon levelled the hill of Moriah to provide a suitable platform for the temple: its natural slope towards the south-east was only corrected by much labour. The site is now occupied by The Dome of the Rock, often erroneously called the Mosque of Omar. It stands exactly over the top of the mount, and encloses a portion of the hill-top left in its native ruggedness. It was probably used as an altar from primeval times. H. V. Morton, in his book, *In the steps of the Master,* writes: 'Lying behind an intricate screen of metal-work is a huge unsmoothed slab of the living rock.... It lies there as out of place and as improbable as a ton of coals in the middle of a drawing-room floor ... It is as if the sharp top of a mountain were pushing its way through the floor of a house'. The top of the mountain it undoubtedly is, and one may suppose that it was deliberately left in its natural state by Solomon when his workmen levelled the rest of the summit.

Of Solomon's temple, and his house which stood south of the temple, no trace remains, but we have good reason to know the source from which he obtained his building stone. Last century, near the Damascus Gate on the north of the city, there was discovered a narrow entrance into subterranean caverns. These were the rock whence the temple was hewn and the hole of the pit whence it was digged. Used as quarries for building stone, they are very extensive and contain a labyrinth of passages. Immense pillars of rock are left standing in the more commodious areas to support the roof. Here without doubt the immense stones for the temple were chiselled and dressed before being built into the fabric on the rock above.

> *'No workman steel, no ponderous axes rung,*
> *Like some tall palm the noiseless fabric sprung'*
> [HEBER]

Some stones are left in the quarries, half cut out and then abandoned. Niches in the rocks indicate where lamps were placed to give light to the masons. The marks of masons abound. It was evident that the dressing of the stones took place in the quarries, for large quantities of stone chippings remain as proof of this. About 1870, Sir Charles Warren sunk shafts through the debris which has accumulated in parts of the temple area. By this means he reached the actual foundations of the original temple and obtained proof that the stones had been lowered into place ready dressed. Had this not been so, stone chips would have been found near the foundation stones, but in the mould close to the wall the only remains discovered were pieces of broken pottery and fragments of ancient lamps for burning fat or oil. The absence of chippings furnishes a remarkable confirmation of the truth of the Old Testament statement [1 *Kings* 6.7]: 'And the house, when it was in building, was built of stone made ready before it was brought thither: so that there was neither hammer nor axe nor any tool of iron heard in the house, while it was in building'.

*

Sir Charles Warren's workmen also discovered letters and marks in red paint on some of the stones. In one case the paint had run to the other side of the stone, which made it clear that the mark had been made before the stone had been laid in position. These marks must have been made by Phoenician masons and were instructions to the actual builders where to lay each stone. Similar marks have been found in ruins in the city of Tyre.

The original entrance to the quarries was probably near the present Damascus Gate, a position which would make the process of moving the stones down to the temple area a comparatively easy one. It is likely that they were run along the side of the Tyropoeon on rollers and brought to their exact position in the wall, so that there would be no occasion to lift them, a matter of considerable difficulty with such 'great stones' as were prepared for the lower courses of the building [1 *Kings* 5.17–18]. One of the stones which has been discovered and measured weighs over 100 tons. It is a gigantic block of limestone, 26 feet long, over 6 feet high, and 7 feet wide.

The extent of Jerusalem as enclosed by its walls has varied through the centuries and forms a difficult study. The Book of *Nehemiah* is specially interesting in this connection. Walls and gates need to be studied together, of course. Scripture conveys substantial information on the subject, but it is not an easy matter to piece together the numerous references and to weave them into an entirely coherent pattern. Certain problems could only be settled by the acquisition of information which has not come down to us, although further digging may throw fresh light on them.

The visitor to Jerusalem today is curious about the so-called Golden Gate facing the Kidron Valley which he sees to be closed. It has been mistakenly linked with the Beautiful gate of the temple mentioned in *Acts* 3.2, and at one time called in Latin 'porta aurea' or 'the golden gate'. For long years the existing gate has been entirely built up, the tradition being that it was closed by the Moslems to show their opposition to the idea that it would be entered by Christ when at His second advent He returns to Zion and turns away ungodliness from Jacob.

JERUSALEM

Lord, in this city Thou didst teach,
Here didst Thou comfort, warn and preach
    Salvation in Thy Name;
And we, as then, may hear Thee still —
May read Thy Word, and know Thy will —
    Ever, as then, the same.

Here cam'st Thou with Thy chosen few,
[Twelve chosen, and yet one untrue],
    Thy passover to keep:
Then, while beneath yon eastern hill
Sorrows of death Thy spirit fill,
    Thy choicest three thrice sleep.

Here, here, prevailed the lawless cry
Of 'Crucify Him — crucify',
    And set the murderer free:
So may each murderous hand and heart,
That now would act a nobler part,
    Come, Prince of Life, to Thee.

And doubly dear that other spot
Without the gate [who knows it not,
    Yet who exactly knows?]
Where to the cross and to the tomb,
To death, to burial Thou didst come;
    Brief triumph of Thy foes.

For where Thou diedst, Thou liv'st again;
That garden nigh that saw Thy pain
    Beheld Thy rising too;
Where late the women saw Thee die,
Spices and balm unheeded lie;
    Thy risen form they view.

Yon eastern mount has seen Thee rise,
Returning to Thy native skies,
    Leaving Thy peace below;
While thoughts of joy within them burn,
Hither Thy chosen ones return,
    Soon through the world to go.

Lord, who the sinner that should die
Freely dost deign to justify,
    And count him for Thine own,
Grant us so now Thy cross to bear,
And Thine own righteousness to wear,
    That we may share Thy throne.

H. B. WHITAKER CHURTON

4

'Jerusalem
...
Jerusalem'

[continued]

I T was a matter of deep satisfaction to me to find that Hezekiah's Tunnel could still be traversed by the tourist and in the
day time. H. V. Morton tells us that, when he went through the
Tunnel, – 'explored it' is his word – he had to go through by
night, as the women around Siloam washed their clothes in the
Pool in the day time and it was essential not to stir up the mud in
the water flowing into it. Morton's dilemma reminds us of the
plight in which Gideon found himself when called to destroy
the altar of Baal : 'Because he feared the men of the city, he could
not do it by day, but did it by night'.

I encountered no difficulty. Probably the women had ceased
to use the Pool. As our party saw it, it did not appear particularly inviting for use as a laundry. Actually several of our party
entered the Tunnel at the Virgin's Fountain and emerged un-
scathed at Siloam. A guide assists tourists and supplies them
with the necessary candles. In anticipation I had myself taken
out from England, specially for this purpose, a strong-beamed
cycle lamp. The water was cold but the atmosphere not unpleasant as, for the moment, we escaped the heat of the sun. The

walls were clammy but there was small need to brush against them: the need was rather to bend sufficiently low to escape the rock above our heads. We could not but admire the skill of Hezekiah's workmen in performing what must certainly have been 'a rush job'; the confined space must have made it difficult to use a pick, yet they had smoothed the walls as they advanced. We could well imagine them, as they worked from opposite ends, taking counsel together in order to achieve a meeting in the heart of the hill. That they succeeded is remarkable. But we may be sure that the king, who knew well how to spread his problems before the Lord, was engaged in daily intercession for the success of the enterprise. Isaiah, too, was in the background.

The water was, for the most part, about knee-deep, but here and there, and especially at the Pool exit, we found it waist-deep. Occasionally we seemed to be walking in slime. It was thrilling in the extreme to feel ourselves, for a moment, back in the 7th century BC, exulting with a Hebrew king and prophet in the success of a most difficult enterprise. We entered, too, into the meaning of the Lord's words addressed to the man with the clay-plastered eyes: 'Go, wash in the Pool of Siloam [which is, by interpretation, Sent]'. I must add, not in my own praise but to the praise of five others, that I was the only male of the party to pass through the waters.

Dr Edward Robinson, who visited Jerusalem in 1838, in his *Biblical Researches in Palestine*, tells how, after entering the tunnel at Gihon, 'We entered and crawled on. . . . Most of the way we could indeed advance upon our hands and knees; yet in several places we could only get forward by lying at full length and dragging ourselves along upon our elbows'. It seems that, in his day, there was a considerable accumulation of sand in the water channel and this made it impossible for a person to progress except by crawling. 'The way seemed interminably long', says Robinson. Not so with ourselves, for we reached Siloam from Gihon in twenty minutes.

Professor Sayce who, as previously mentioned, copied and translated the Siloam inscription, in his *Reminiscences* follows reference to the Tunnel by a paragraph which is worthy of quotation: 'I lunched one day with the British Consul [i.e. in Jerusalem] and noticed that there was a vacant place at his table. He was a very efficient consul, a good scholar, and an authority upon ancient art, and I was therefore much surprised at being told that the vacant place was always there, as my host expected that it would be occupied by our Lord at His second coming. It is hard for those who live in Jerusalem to escape the contagion of its religious element.'

On another occasion we walked through the Via Dolorosa and saw the so-called Nine Stations of the Cross. The buildings we visited were not without interest, but it was far from easy to piece together in a coherent pattern which made sense to the mind, all the information about ancient houses and palaces, stairways and other structures, which made up the Jerusalem of Christ's day. Large paving stones marked with soldiers' games were pointed out to us as we were told that on that very spot must have stood the various buildings used by the Roman garrison in the city.

Our visit to the Dome of the Rock with its Moslem buildings, the chief of which was the ornate mosque with its magnificent dome visible from afar, included the sight of the peak of rock previously mentioned where must have stood the Jewish altar of burnt offering. As we stood there, of necessity in our bare or our stockinged feet, surveying the product of architectural skill and realizing that the 'faith' which it represented was a principal rival to Christianity, we called to mind that it was here that Melchisedek, the priest-king of Abraham's day, had reigned in glorious state, and shown forth in his unique person something of the wonders which attached to Him of whom it was later to be spoken, 'The Lord hath sworn and will not repent, Thou art a priest for ever after the order of Melchisedek' [*Psalm* 110.4]. Here, too, Abraham, the father of the faithful, had 'offered up his only-begotten son', and received him [in a figure] back again from the dead. Here Solomon had reared his temple. Here in another and a later temple the veil had been rent from the top to the bottom.

We could not but feel awed into silence. But in our minds ran the thought that we were standing in a fane where the deity of the Messiah, and the once-for-all atonement He had effected by His death, are denied and hated, while the spurious claims of another are exalted to the skies. It is even claimed that, from this spot, Mahomet ascended to heaven, carried there on the back of el-Baruk, his miraculous steed. Two hairs from Mahomet's beard are, it is claimed, preserved hereabouts also. Prophecies of the future accompany the wonders, as that, for instance, 'at the last day the Kaaba of Mecca will come to the Dome of the Rock, for here will resound the blast of the trumpet announcing the judgment. God's throne will then be set up on the Rock,'. 'Alas', commented the Pentecostalist member of our party, 'They see in the Lord Jesus no beauty that they should desire Him. He is still despised and rejected of men'. With such a thought we passed again out into the sunlight, retrieved our shoes, crossed the vast paved area surrounding the Dome, admired the mimosas in full flower, witnessed certain Moslem ablutions, and found our way to the underground area called Solomon's stables.

The stables did not detain us long, despite their refreshing coolness. The guide showed us, by means of certain mural features, how the floor level had altered through the centuries.

Reconstruction must have taken place on at least one occasion. He pointed to holes in the stone pillars which had obviously been made for the tethering of animals. We were thus duly impressed with a fresh aspect of 'Solomon in all his glory', but wondered why he had not paid more attention to the words of warning in the Mosaic law: 'The king whom the Lord thy God shall choose shall not multiply horses to himself' [*Deut.* 17.15–16], and Solomon had done just that! A similar warning concerning multiplying wives and storing up silver and gold immediately follows: and here again Solomon was grievously at fault.

The site of Bethesda interested us much, as it so clearly conformed to the requirements of the Gospel narrative [*John* 5.1–9]. It is situated not far from the gate named after Stephen, the Christian faith's proto-martyr, and has been exposed to view fairly recently. Its character vividly suggests the existence of the five colonnades or porches mentioned by John, and the lying in wait by multitudes of invalids could easily be envisaged.

Another of the authentic sites of the city is found just below the Church of St Peter Gallicantu [Cock-crowing]. A flight of much-worn irregular stone steps, abnormally wide, leads from near the Pool of Siloam to a spot which is claimed to be the site of the House of the high priest Caiaphas. Here, we were told, Peter's denial of his Master took place. Inside the church we were shown a depressing dungeon into which, from an aperture in the wall above, a guard could keep watch on the prisoners in confinement. We thought of similar holes [for what better can they be called?] in the Tower of London and similar places.

*

The one site in Jerusalem, however, which gave us more pleasure than any other was the Garden Tomb situated near the Damascus Gate. I am quite incompetent to discuss the probabilities and improbabilities involved in the problem of the site of the crucifixion and of Joseph of Arimathaea's garden, but a visit to the Garden Tomb is the most rewarding thing within the city. Whether or not it is the exact site of happenings the like of which neither angels nor men have seen, it seems to correspond so nearly with such inspired words as we have to guide us that we could find rest in the identification; and, archaeological considerations apart [and these necessarily depend upon experts who contend with experts], it wears the marks of reality. It is remarkable that, in the heart of modern Jerusalem, in a spot which, clearly enough, may well have been outside the city wall of two thousand years ago, there should be found a rock-hewn tomb in a garden wearing all the signs of undoubted antiquity, and near to a low cliff-face which bears still the outward aspect of 'the place of a skull'.

The collation of Gospel passages which bear upon the matter has convinced some of the experts that there is much to be said in favour of General Gordon's identification of 'the place of a skull' [every time we use the word 'Calvary' we give utterance to the matter], and upon this factor the evidence partly hinges. If Golgotha was so named because a certain low cliff near the Damascus Gate bears a resemblance in eye sockets, nose and mouth, to a human skull, and if the appearance of the present site is little changed from that of two thousand years ago, then the case is a strong one. But notoriously, the combination of an 'if' with an 'if' in matters historic and archaeological is unsafe evidence on which to base firm conclusions.

I must not attempt to argue the matter further. But if the reader ever follows our steps to Jerusalem, I think he will agree with me that Gordon's Calvary, surmounted though it is by a Moslem cemetery, and under-girded [so to speak] by a noisy bus station, is a place which, together with the neighbouring Garden Tomb, lends itself admirably to meditation on the event which 'shook the earth and veiled the sun'. That Christ suffered, the Just for the unjust, to bring us to God; that a site outside the gate was the decreed place of His suffering; that He was buried in a near-by garden and in a newly-excavated tomb; and that on the third day He rose again from the dead with the power of an endless life, is the most stupendous series of events – and virtually one event – not only in history but in eternity. It stands as the 'miracle of time, God's own sacrifice complete'. The precise geographical spot matters little in comparison of the fact itself. But if identification is at all possible, then the site of the present Garden Tomb seems to meet all the biblical requirements.

The Garden itself is kept in order by skilful hands. We saw a gardener at work at the time of our visit. The warden[1] and his American wife welcome visitors and link well-chosen words about the actual site with a message which conveys the essence of the Gospel to all and sundry, whether Christian or otherwise. One has to stoop slightly to enter the rocky recess in which Joseph intended his own body to find sepulture. No stone for closing the tomb is to be seen, nor is there any obvious groove into which such a stone might have fitted. But we can well believe that in such a garden as this, the reverent hands of Joseph and Nicodemus laid the bruised body of the Lord to rest; and in such a garden at deep dawn on the first day of the

[1] We much regret to learn that during the Israeli–Arab conflict of June, 1967, the warden was shot and subsequently died.

new week, the event took place which marked the beginning
of the new creation.

*

Lord Jesus Christ, Thou dwell'st in highest Heaven,
    Th' embosomed Son of Love,
From everlasting days God's own begotten,
    While angels all above
Chanted Thy praise, First Cause of all creation,
    Earth's cornerstone not laid,
Nor Adam, first of men, nor any nation
    By Thy strong hand yet made.

But such Thy love to men, when guilty sinners,
    And such Thy heart's deep grace,
That they might of eternal life be winners,
    Thou didst not hide Thy face
From all the shame that came through incarnation
    Nor from the pain and strife;
Thou camst to earth and wrought a full salvation,
    Thy death the gate to life.

The agony and woe of Thy deep passion
    The olive garden showed:
But such the wonders of Thy great compassion,
    Thou still didst tread the road
Which led to Golgotha and dereliction –
    All seemed but grief and loss –
But to Thy Church what wealth of benediction
    Resulted from Thy cross!

The third day came – 'tis in the Scriptures numbered –
    And Thou didst leave the bed
Wherein Thy sacred body safe had slumbered
    When Thou wast with the dead.
The grave could then no longer hold Thee sleeping,
    Loosed were the bonds and pain,

For Thou, O Lord of life, hadst in Thy keeping
*   The keys of death's domain.*

And now all power most rightfully is given
*   To Thee, my Sovereign Lord;*
All other power in earth or hell or heaven
*   Falls down before Thy Word.*
And every knee shall homage render to Thee,
*   And every tongue confess*
That Thou, the Christ, dost reign in kingly glory,
*   And perfect righteousness.*

*

As we sat, on one occasion in the Garden, and pondered the event, a small tortoise appeared and crossed the sunlit path with laboured steps and slow. Thus slow are we, at best, to grasp the eternal import of the transactions of earth's most tremendous days, but upon them, by grace, our hopes for time and eternity depend: 'Begotten again unto a lively hope by the resurrection of Jesus Christ from the dead . . . who is gone into Heaven and is on the right hand of God, angels and authorities and powers being made subject unto Him' [1 *Peter* 1.3 & 3.21–22].

We visited the Garden Tomb and its simple sublimities twice, and twice left it to return to the world of the merchantmen, the street vendor, the bazaar, the shoe-cleaner, the motor-horn-blower, the Arab and the Moslem who surged around its walls. Here were sellers of olive-wood camels, strung together on chains, of cakes and bread so different in appearance from the cakes and loaves of the West, of fruits strange to the overseas visitor, of antiques without number in wood and metal. Here were men puffing solemnly at hookahs, men entering into heated debate, men sipping very black coffee, men indolent, men busy; here in fact were many illustrations of oriental city life. Here, too, were the women of the city, abundantly clothed [for the most part] in 'divers colours of needlework, of divers colours of needlework on both sides', 'meet for the necks' of the daughters of Jerusalem. We noted that even when at work in the fields of the land, as was often the case, under the broiling sun, women's garments were ample and usually of ankle-length. Not for Arab women or Jewesses, except maybe in such places as Tel Aviv, the unbecoming brevity of western dress! Over some of the streets in Mea Shearim, the most religious quarter of the Jewish part of the city [which we saw later], are to be seen notices in Hebrew and English, conspicuously displayed, speaking thus:

> *Jewish daughters, the Torah obligates you to dress with modesty. We do not tolerate people passing through our streets immodestly dressed [Committee for Guarding Modesty].*

*

Outside the walls of the city and across the valley of the Kidron, our visit to Gethsemane – the olive press – showed it as the photographs we had seen led us to expect. Palestine is the land of the olive tree; its limestone hills appear to suit it down to the ground. It is found in all parts of the land. When we visited northern Galilee we saw square miles of olives, mostly newly planted. When we remarked on their abundance to our guide he referred us to Moses' blessing on Asher, recorded in *Deuteronomy* 33.24, 'Let him dip his foot in oil'. The apostle who writes to the Romans takes the olive tree as a most suitable figure for the nation of Israel, and speaks of the 'root and fatness of the olive tree' [*Romans* 11].

C. H. Spurgeon, who made close observation of the olive trees growing at Mentone on the Riviera, delighted to wander among them and preached several sermons on their beauties as indicative of various graces in the believer. Perhaps it will not be accounted an unpardonable digression if I quote from one of them:

Truth to tell, it is not the most shapely of the sons of the forest. It is not a tree which would at once strike the beholder with admiration, like some giant oak, or lofty elm; nor charm him with its elegance, like a weeping willow; nor astonish him with its grandeur, like a cedar of Lebanon. In order to perceive its beauty you must linger a little. You must look, and look again; and then, if you do not at least feel a deep respect for the olive, and a quiet delight in its beauty, it must be because you are not of a thoughtful spirit, or else because you have little poetry in your soul. The more familiar you become with the olive tree, the more will you take pleasure in it.

The colour of the olive foliage is a grey green. It belongs to the same family as the ash, and is of a somewhat similar colour, only of a lighter green, one side of the leaf being much paler than the other. I have recently watched olive trees almost every day, for three months, but they always appeared somewhat different, varying in colour and tint as the day was cloudless, overcast, or decidedly wet. Even the position of the sun caused a change in their appearance and a little wind, turning up the silver side of the leaves, presented a new phase of beauty. After a shower of rain, the green appeared predominant; and on a hot and dusty day the grey was in the ascendant. In the evening they some-times seemed slaty or drab, and another time they wore a silvery sheen. Like certain other colours which vary with the light, the tint of the olive leaf is peculiar in yielding to its sur-roundings. It does seem as if it followed the mood of nature and blended it with its own. I do not think I am fanciful, but it seemed to me that this tree was in wonderful sympathy with the weather, the sun, the sky, the clouds, the morning and the evening.

Olive trees are wondrously varied. The twists and turns of the branches, the singular way in which they grow down where you think they can never grow, and the equally remarkable way in which they do not grow where you think they should, the curious shapes and the shapeless shapes that they take I cannot describe to you. Sometimes some of the branches seem as if they were turned to serpents, coiling themselves around the bigger branches. The olive trees always appear to me to be in an agony, twisting and turning like one in excruciating pain, as if they remembered the griefs and woes of Him who sweat as it were great drops of blood when He agonized beneath the shade of the olives in Gethsemane.

The trunk of the olive is often split into many separate parts, and each part seems to be full of vitality. You scarcely ever see one that appears to be entire; they are rent and torn as though sundered by volcanic eruptions and they are turned into all manner of shapes so that no one of them is like its fellows. Here and there one sees a young tree that seems, for a while, to have a definite shape, and to grow up in some sort of comely form; but you see another, by its side, smaller still, which has not grown three feet above the ground before it takes a twist, and goes down again, and then comes up again once more, forming letters something like a W or an S or a V, but never reaching the shape that you would have thought it might have done. The individuality in the olive tree is a part of the charm of the olive grove.

The olive tree is full of life, but it seems to be always a struggling life. As you get a glimpse of some olive trees, you say to yourself, 'That tree must have had a hard time of it'. The gnarled and knotted old trunk is split up just as if an axe had been driven through it. You can see the white wood inside, and on the surface the rugged bark appears in places as if it were rotten, yet you find that it is still alive. Then you see the branches that grow out of these various divisions of the trunk twisting and twirling and wriggling in and out as if they lived in perpetual agony, for they have to draw oil out of the flinty rock. It would involve much hard labour for men to accomplish that task, yet the olive tree is continually doing it, yielding the precious oil which not only makes the face of man to shine, but which supplies him with food and light the whole year round. This the olive tree often does in a sterile soil where there appears to be no nourishment for it whatever. It seems as if the olive tree, though always in an agony, is always full of life. It is not an easy matter to kill an olive tree. Even if you hew it down, yet leave the stump or a portion of its roots in the ground, it will begin to sprout and grow again. If you let the tree stand for a thousand years or more, it will still bring forth fruit in old age; and when it is at last worn out and decayed, its children will have grown up into a fruitful grove all around it.

Thus far Spurgeon, quoted, for brevity's sake, without the spiritual application which he makes of the olive tree and its fruit.

Even more than the vine and the figtree, the olive tree is a fitting emblem of Israel and its land. Let neighbouring lands glory, if they will, in a very different kind of oil, but in Israel's case we have the prophetic assertion that 'his beauty shall be as the olive tree' [*Hos.* 14.6]. Of olive wood were made the cherubim in the temple's holy of holies; olive oil supplied the light of the golden candlestick; the labour of the olive filled the bowl of the candlestick in Zechariah's prophetic vision. But we must turn again to Gethsemane.

The trees of Gethsemane are certainly ancient and worthy of respect, but the present-day garden lacks the retired character of the retreat to which the Lord 'oft-times resorted with his disciples'. There are two such gardens actually, one linked with the Roman Church and the other with the Orthodox. The former Church, immediately behind its garden, displays

the rock upon which, it is claimed, the Lord prostrated Himself
in agonizing prayer. It is one of the darkest ecclesiastical buildings I have ever entered. The windows seem designed to
exclude rather than to admit the light

I myself found what I can only describe as my own private
olive garden. It happened in this way. Leaving the olives of the
Roman and Orthodox gardens I walked along the Kidron
valley towards what goes by the name of Absalom's tomb [or
monument], a conspicuous landmark, though not occupying
an elevated position. To the right of the tomb the ground fell
sharply away and I noticed that olives were growing there in
abundance. Clambering down the slope I found myself in the
dry concrete conduit made for the Kidron brook, passed
through an open gateway over the conduit and was soon
among the olives. Younger by far than those of the 'official'
Gethsemane, they provided shade and privacy, and among
them for a little while I sat alone pondering the events which
were the prelude to Calvary.

> ' 'Twas here the Lord of Life appeared,
> And sighed and groaned and prayed and feared;
> Bore all incarnate God could bear,
> With strength enough, and none to spare.
>
> 'Backwards and forwards thrice He ran,
> As if He sought some help from man,
> Or wished at least they would condole
> ['Twas all they could] His tortured soul.
>
> 'Mysterious conflict! dark disguise!
> Hid from all creatures' peering eyes.
> Angels astonished viewed the scene,
> And wonder yet what all could mean.'

JOSEPH HART

'Gethsemane, the olive press, and why so-called let Christians guess': Sacred spot indeed! I returned to the hotel after climbing the steep rocky path up the slopes of Olivet and taking another view of the city from this vantage point.

*

Our one Lord's Day in Jerusalem had its joys and sorrows. The sorrows came first, and strangely, from a quarter from which we expected the joy. The place was the Y.M.C.A., the occasion the morning service. To begin with, it was alarming to find the notice board of the building largely devoted to advertisements of ballet dancing and theatricals. Some might hold it to be in bad taste to mention such a matter, but conscience must be given its voice. The large light and airy hall where, I suppose, entertainment was the normal order of the weekdays, was now the scene of a fifty-minutes' service. It was long since I had listened to such a wretched discourse as was given by an American Methodist. So much did its theology seem to be of the 'God is dead' variety, that it was a relief to reach the concluding benediction. I may be thought an extremist, but I was so much troubled that, when coffee was freely offered in the canteen immediately after the service, I felt too much in harmony with the injunction given to the unnamed 'disobedient prophet' of 1 *Kings* 13.9 to partake of it.

A few of our party next attended a second morning service in an upper room where the Baptist Church of Jerusalem carries on its worship. The service was in striking contrast to that which we had just attended. The Word was faithfully ministered by the Lebanese pastor from *Zechariah* 13.6 ['What are these wounds in thine hands? Then he shall answer, Those with which I was wounded in the house of my friends']. Our spirits were revived, not to say comforted. Dutch and Amer-

[79]

ican believers were present as well as a few folk resident in Jerusalem. The Americans were invited to speak briefly of a work of tract and Bible distribution which they were pursuing in the Middle East.

The experiences of the day produced a powerful reminder of the fact that there are two Jerusalems; 'that which is now, and is in bondage with her children; and that which is above, which is free, and which is the mother of us all' [i.e. all true believers in Christ Jesus]. So speaks *Galatians* 4.25–26. Bondage belongs to the one, freedom to the other. Sad indeed it is that multitudes dwelling in the earthly 'city of God' know nothing of what it is to 'dwell in the secret place of the most High' and 'to abide under the shadow of the Almighty'! And nothing but the Gospel once wrought out in this very city, the 'city of the great King', and proclaimed in the power of the Holy Ghost sent down from heaven, is sufficient to heal the grievous sore of the centuries, and to fit Jerusalem for her future name as given by the prophet, 'Jehovah-Shammah', 'the Lord is there' [*Ezek*. 48.35]!

TEARS FOR JERUSALEM

Jerusalem, Jerusalem ! enthronèd once on high,
Thou favoured home of God on earth, thou heaven below the sky.
Now brought to bondage with thy sons, a curse and grief to see:
Jerusalem, Jerusalem! our tears shall flow for thee.

Oh, hadst thou known thy day of grace, and flocked beneath the wing
Of Him who called thee lovingly, thine own anointed King;
Then had the tribes of all the world gone up thy pomp to see,
And glory dwelt within thy gates, and all thy sons been free.

'And who art thou that mournest us?' replied the ruin grey,
'And fear'st not rather that thyself may prove a castaway?'
I am a dried and abject branch, my place is given to thee,
But woe to every barren graft of thy wild olive tree!

'Our day of grace is sunk in night, our time of mercy spent,
For heavy was my children's crime, and strange their punishment;
Yet gaze not idly on our fall, but, sinner, warnèd be,
Who sparèd not His chosen seed may send His wrath on thee.

'Our day of grace is sunk in night, thy noon is in its prime,
O turn and seek thy Saviour's face in this accepted time;
So, Gentile, may Jerusalem a lesson prove to thee,
And in the New Jerusalem thy home for ever be!'

[BISHOP] REGINALD HEBER

5

From
Jerusalem
to
Samaria

T HIS chapter will cover certain of the visits we made while
in Jordan, to places other than Jerusalem. The first was to
the country north of the capital city. I had hoped that it would
have been possible to visit the site of ancient Gibeon, the city
where lived the folk who deceived Joshua and entered into a
pact with the Israelites, after which [not being slain] they became 'hewers of wood and drawers of water for the congrega-
tion and for the altar of the Lord' [*Josh*. 9.27]. At a later date the
Pool of Gibeon becomes prominent in Bible story, but in rather
mysterious fashion: David's men met Abner's men and engaged
in 'very sore battle' [2 *Sam*. 2.17] after sitting for a while on
opposite sides of the Pool. About twelve years ago the mystery
was solved by American archaeologists who excavated a vast
rock-cut circular pit, 36 feet in diameter and 33 feet in depth.
This was the Pool, long covered with earth. Presumably it
never held water, for the excavators discovered a winding staircase leading from its base to the water-table fifty feet below,
where the ancient inhabitants of Gibeon had carved out a large
room for collecting the precious liquid. The 'dig' established

beyond a doubt the special renown which the Gibeonites had anciently achieved as 'drawers of water'. The labour put into the original work must have been immense. Water still flows into the room out of the hard limestone of which the entire area is composed. From top to bottom of the water-system there are no less than 158 steps cut out of the rock. Water carrying must have been a laborious task in days of old, for, in many cases, cities were built on hills, and, naturally, springs of water were normally found in the valleys below them.

We by-passed Gibeon, only a few miles to the north of Jerusalem. Our car-drivers did not wish to diverge from the highway, so we could not manage a view of this fascinating spot. Instead we drove on over the limestone hills which seemed much to resemble those of Derbyshire, except that they were often terraced almost from base to summit. Small culti-vated fields, occasionally green but often scorched to brown even at this early part of the year, came now and again into sight. Almonds, apricots, figs and olives seemed to grow in abundance.

Our first stop was at Beeroth, reputedly the spot where Joseph and Mary realized that 'the child Jesus' was not to be found among the company returning from keeping Passover at Jerusalem, and from which they retraced their steps seeking Him [*Luke* 2.44]. We could well believe that this was the spot and that it ranked as 'a day's journey' from the capital city, even though it hardly seemed more than five or six miles from it. It was probably the case that the first day's journey of the return was shorter than that of later days owing to the delays occas-ioned by preparations for the journey back to distant homes. Beeroth still boasts a public water supply, a vital qualification for a travellers' stopping place.

Nowadays Beeroth can almost be reckoned a suburb of Jeru-

salem, and we were told that King Hussein himself had a residence there. The building material has a close resemblance to
Cotswold stone.

Travelling north we halted at a spot from which a good view
of Bethel is to be obtained, and recollections of a fugitive, a
stone pillow, a ladder, and a promise came vividly to mind.
Bethel's later evil reputation as the focus of Jeroboam's calf
worship seemed utterly incongruous with the sunlit scene of
peace which feasted our eyes. But it remains true that the vile-
ness of man can pollute nature's loveliest setting. Sodom's
awful excesses were perpetrated in what Scripture describes
as 'the garden of the Lord' [*Gen.* 13.10].

*

From Bethel we moved on to Sychar, 'near to the parcel of
ground that Jacob gave to his son Joseph' [*John* 4.5]. On the
one side was Mount Ebal from which, to an assembled nation
in the days of Joshua, were read the curses of the law; opposite
was Mount Gerizim from which the blessings promised to
obedience were rehearsed. The solemn Amen of the tribes, six
here and six there, seemed to echo still from the confronting
hills. Mountains have been silent witnesses of the goodness
and severity of a covenant-keeping God.

Between the hills is the well which lies at the very centre of
Gospel story. Its natural beauty is obscured by the building
which now covers it. Even so, it was an experience of sheer
delight to stand and sit by turns on the stones where the Lord
confessed His thirst to a sinner far from God and made His
physical need the text of a discourse which for eternity, and not
only for time, speaks the fundamentals of a truly spiritual worship. Here too He revealed in plain direct statement His
Messiahship – 'I that speak unto thee am He'. Here the un-

named woman of Samaria learned the secret of eternal life. We
certainly do not do violence to the narrative or force it beyond
its legitimate bounds if we put into her lips a prayer penned
centuries later in a far-distant land:

> *'Thou of life the Fountain art,*
> *Freely let me take of Thee;*
> *Spring Thou up within my heart,*
> *Rise to all eternity.'*

The bucket descended into the well time and time again, and
the assembled company sipped with awe mingled with joy.
Our leader suggested that we should sing two verses of Horatius Bonar's hymn; 'I heard the voice of Jesus say, Come unto
Me and rest', including the lines:

> *'I heard the voice of Jesus say:*
> *Behold, I freely give*
> *The living water; thirsty one,*
> *Stoop down and drink and live!*
> *I came to Jesus and I drank*
> *Of that life-giving stream;*
> *My thirst was quenched, my soul revived,*
> *And now I live in Him.'*

It was an unforgettable experience to sing these words at the
very spot – no mistake about that! – where the Lord of Life
'being wearied with His journey, sat thus on the well'.

It may here be mentioned that, when a brother of Horatius
Bonar visited the well in 1839, his Bible fell accidentally into
the water and was, of course, irrecoverable. The incident is
recorded in the following words in the Narrative of a Mission
to the Jews from the Church of Scotland in 1839:

'The guide removed a large stone that covers the mouth of
the low vault built over the well; and then thrusting himself

through the narrow aperture, invited Mr Bonar to follow. This he accordingly did; and in the act of descending, his Bible escaping from his breast-pocket fell into the well, and was soon heard plunging in the water far below. The guide made very significant signs that it could not be recovered, "for the well is deep" ... Mr Calhoun, who was here recently, found it seventy-five feet deep, with ten or twelve feet of water. In all the other wells and fountains which we saw in this valley, the water is within reach of the hand, but in this one the water seems never to rise high. This is one of the clear evidences that it is really the Well of Jacob, for at this day it would require what it required in the days of our Lord, an "antlema", "something to draw with," for it was deep'. [Actually the remnants of this Bible were recovered four years later when another Scottish visitor to Sychar employed a Samaritan to descend the well].

*

Not far from the well, between Ebal and Gerizim, lies the village of Nablus, a name which appears to be a corruption of Neapolis, one of the rare examples of a place which has exchanged its ancient Semitic name for one of Roman origin. It is the site of ancient Shechem, and therefore a veritable mine of biblical history. But hard it is to realize that these hills and ridges, so completely rural in character at the present day, were the places where so many events chronicled in sacred history were enacted. It was at Shechem that all Israel was gathered to make Rehoboam, Solomon's son, king; here it was that Jeroboam promoted the debates which resulted in the separation of the ten tribes from the two, when 'Israel rebelled against the house of David unto this day' [1 *Kings* 12.19]. 'Our fathers worshipped in this mountain', said the woman at the well, doubtless pointing as she spoke to the spot on Mount Gerizim where stood the temple which, in Samaritan eyes, rivalled that in Jerusalem. Whatever outward religious grandeur the area once possessed, its tinsel glory has long since departed, and the present village, miserable enough as it is to all outward appearance, houses the remnants of the ancient Samaritan sect.

Escorted by the inevitable children, we climbed the steps giving access to the unkempt little synagogue, to find a couple of white-surpliced red-turbaned bearded priests holding to view their scroll of the Pentateuch which, they informed us, was the oldest book in the world, dating from a few years after the time of Moses himself! It was permitted to make contact by placing a finger upon its hoary characters, in return for which privilege a collecting box lay close to hand. Instead of taking advantage of the latter's proximity, I decided to purchase a small metal replica of the scroll and its rollers, imagining that the small portion of Hebrew exposed to view within it indicated the presence of the whole of the Samaritan Pentateuch. But later I discovered to my chagrin that the side rolls which I had supposed to be fully biblical were nothing more than empty cast-off sheets from a philatelic album. It cost me ten shillings!

From Nablus we descended from the heights in a north-westerly direction for five or six miles and arrived where we could see something of the 'glorious beauty which is on the head of the fat valley'. Isaiah's description [28.4] refers to the city of Samaria founded by Omri, who decided to move the capital of the Northern Kingdom from Tirzah – it had previously been moved there from Shechem – to this truly pleasant spot. Its present name is Sebaste [Greek for Augusta]. As a military site it was sufficiently strong to sustain a siege at the hands of the Assyrians lasting three years. Its fall in 721 BC brought to an end the idolatrous kingdom of Israel, the ten tribes then passing into captivity and exile. In ancient days the hill, as viewed from the military angle, must have possessed exceptional natural strength, and it is not difficult to imagine the satisfaction that must have filled Omri's heart as its defences and the walls which he raised became a substitute for trust in the living God. Little wonder that Amos warned his generation, 'Woe to them that trust in the mountain of Samaria' [6.1], while Micah prophesied, 'I will make Samaria as an heap of the field . . . and I will pour down the stones thereof into the valley' [1.6]. The word was literally fulfilled in its season.

We made a tour of the site. Imagination filled the surrounding valleys with the hosts of Shalmanezer which, drawn there as God's avengers, awaited the surrender of the doomed city, just as, in a later day, the hosts of a Babylonian king filled the Hinnom and the Kidron valleys in daily expectation of the subjugation of the city of God. Omri had built an immensely strong wall to enclose the hill of Samaria, and Ahab, his son, had further strengthened the place by constructing a casemated wall around the hill-top. The most impressive part of the ruins which we saw were the foundations of Omri's wall. It is believed that he had the help of Phoenician builders in its construction. Ahab, Scripture tells us, built an ivory house for himself, [1 *Kings* 22.39], by which we are doubtless to understand a house whose ornamentation was in ivory; and when archaeologists got to work in recent times they discovered in the ruins fragments of first-rate ivory carvings. Of course we ourselves saw nothing of these, but we saw enough to remind us of a king long remembered for the evil statutes he promulgated [*Micah* 6.16] and of his son of whom it is ominously written that 'there was none like unto Ahab, which did sell himself to work wickedness in the sight of the Lord' [1 *Kings* 21.25].

It was in a rebuilt Samaria, that Philip came preaching the Gospel, which caused 'great joy in that city' [*Acts* 8.8]. Pleasant it was to think that the abominations linked with the worship of the Omri-Ahab period had given place at this later date to the joy of the Lord!

In the midst of the ruins of these ancient cities, one built upon another after the fashion of the Orient, we were shown what purported to be the tomb of John the Baptist, but how it was that John's body came to be brought here for burial we could not understand, for his ancestry belonged to 'the hill country of Judaea' south of Jerusalem, and his death took place in the gloomy fortress of Machaerus, east of the Dead Sea.

Descending the hill and returning to our cars we found an Arab with his supercilious camel – all camels look supercilious – demanding a fee from tourists for the privilege of taking his photograph, a polite youth selling booklets about Sebaste, a goat with a broken bandaged leg, and a sense that, if privilege was in question, we had exercised it abundantly [yet not abundantly enough] in surveying one of the most historic sites of Holy Writ. Talking to our driver on the return journey to Jerusalem, I learned that animosity between Jews and Arabs still smouldered fiercely, that most Arabs had families of nine or ten children, that English was the second language after Arabic in the schools, and that petrol was four shillings a gallon!

*

We had reason to admire the system of performing scholastic homework adopted by some at least of the nation's children. The bedroom window of our hotel on Olivet gave us a view of the slopes of the mountain and a close-up view of the gardens of the haphazardly-scattered houses, several of which appeared rather superior to the great mass of the dwellings which occupy the hill-slopes of the district. The house nearest the hotel possessed a garden orderly and ample. Each morning, often before six, we could watch a girl of about fourteen pacing between the trees as she conned her lesson book. We had the notion that it was necessary for her to memorize the book's contents, and the further notion that this was possibly the only book basic to her education, except perhaps the Koran. I handled it on one occasion and discovered that it covered almost all the subjects of the curriculum. On most occasions the girl's steady pacing continued over two hours. One morning I made it my business from the other side of the garden wall to speak to her and to ask whether she would like me to send her a lesson book from England. She expressed pleasure at the suggestion, telling me that her special liking was for History. Her name was Wahebia. My few words with her led to a small concentration around me of similar scholars whose preferences were, in Rihab's case for Teacher-training, and in Basima's for Science. An older youth who joined the animated group informed me that he was a University student and that he aimed at becoming a politician. At his request, though a little reluctantly, I entered his near-by home, but retreated in some haste and embarrassment when I discovered that his relations of both sexes were still a-bed. One of them was listening to a transistor radio. The house had two rooms and a tiny kitchen.

The people of Jordan seem extraordinarily fond of the radio. The various cars in which we travelled were all fitted with radio sets, and our drivers appeared to take it for granted that we and they alike were bound to appreciate the cacaphony of pop music and of much else that could only grate on our ears. Once when I intimated that, for my part, I should like it turned off, the driver seemed almost hurt by my suggestion. Possibly he regarded its use as one of the privileges belonging to his job. Even the poorest families possessed sets, or so it seemed. Bedouin huts resounded with them; and even on the top of a 'high place' of ancient sacrifice, up in the high hills beyond Petra, it was still the same. For better or for worse radio has spread its tentacles afar.

BETHANY

'To the hill-side
Here hid among her trees, a village clings,
Roof above roof uprising; white the walls,
And whiter still by contrast, and those roofs,
Broad sunny platforms, strewed with ripening grain,
And peopled thick with gaily coloured groups,
Housing the golden produce of their toil.
But higher still, the patient labourer
Contends undaunted with the stony waste,
Wresting his hard-won harvest, till the soil
Mocks his vain fruitless efforts, and alone
Some wandering olive, or unsocial fig,
Amid the broken rocks which bound my path,
Snatches scant nurture from the crevic'd stone.

And this is Bethany! and here abode
The favoured family whom Jesus loved;
To whose warm, humble welcome, 'twas His wont,
Tracking the path but now I passed along,
Oft to retire from foes and wavering friends.

'Twas here His verdict full acquittal gave,
And high approval of the glowing zeal,
Which, for the 'better part' forbore to share
A sister's weak anxieties. 'Twas here
He wept, in tender sympathy with woes,
By His command so soon to be absorbed
In grateful joy. Here, by His power divine,
Bade death release its prey, the untrammell'd soul
Return to earth, and gave a living proof
And pledge of future immortality.

And when, His work all ended, He prepared
To re-ascend His throne, this way He led
His sorrowing followers for a last farewell.

It seems a humble village, few its homes,
And few and poor its dwellers; cottage roofs,
Except one simple turret, are they all!
Yet save the neighbouring city, it were hard,
If Palestine were searched, to find a spot
On which the Christian traveller should muse
With fonder interest, than Bethany.

[Quoted from Walks about Jerusalem
W. H. BARTLETT 1844]

6
Bethany
Bethlehem
Hebron
Petra

IT was inevitable that we should take Bethlehem in our stride. It might have seemed practicable to do so in the most literal sense, for its distance from Jerusalem is only six miles; but the meandering character of the Israel-Jordan frontier necessitated a detour which lengthened the journey to nine miles. Then, too, Europeans have always to reckon with the heat of the day. On the other hand, the elevation of the whole district – Jerusalem is 2500 feet above sea level – gives the walker a feeling of exhilaration which is lacking in lower regions. But where cars are available, who can hold out against upholstered ease?

Our first stop was at Bethany ['the place or house of figs'], 'the town of Mary and her sister Martha'. At first sight it seemed a delectable little village, and like its immense neighbour, 'beautiful for situation'. Obviously it held for us one spot of intense interest; not a house, for who could expect what was doubtless a humble habitation to survive the ravages of two thousand years? But caves, being natural, tend to escape the 'tooth of time'. And in this case the grave we sought was 'a cave, and a stone lay upon it '[*John* 11.38]. It may be wondered how it comes about that only one of the Four Gospels includes the story of the raising of the man who had been dead four days before He who is the Resurrection and the Life appeared in living person before his burial place, but this does not present the slightest hindrance to belief in the amazing event that Bethany and Jerusalem now witnessed. We add 'Jerusalem', for John makes it clear that 'many of the Jews' from the capital city were present in Bethany to comfort the sorrowing sisters when the miracle took place.

The raising of Lazarus is wrought inextricably into the story of the last days of Christ's earthly ministry, and shares as fully in historical authenticity as does the resurrection of the Messiah Himself. Already and elsewhere the Lord had demonstrated His power over death. His 'Talitha cumi' had resulted in the restoration of a girl of twelve to her sorrowing parents. Outside Nain He had restored to a widowed mother a young man being carried to the place of burial. But at Bethany, not death alone, but the insatiable grave, which never says 'It is enough', met its Conqueror: 'O grave, where is thy victory?' At Bethany, in the one particular case, the Lord indicated what would happen to every true follower of His 'in the resurrection at the last day'. Then, not a groaning but a glorified Saviour, in the dew of eternal youth, will utter the word which will be heard by all who 'sleep in Jesus'. Putting on immortality, and with bodies made like unto His glorious body, they, together with living believers, will be 'caught up' to be for ever with the Lord. No need at that day for stones of sepulchres to be rolled away, nor need for others to loose the resurrected and let them go!

At Bethany, however, the Lord humbled Himself to regard the needs of those still in the flesh. Slowly we climbed to that part of the present town where it is claimed that the grave of

Lazarus is still to be seen. To the right were dwellings which no Englishman would care to call his domicile. Poultry, scratching with vigour in the dust, reminded us that we ourselves are still of the earth, earthy. And here again, always attractive to our eyes, was the supercilious camel. This particular specimen had learned the art of raising its head aloft with a bottle of mineral waters held firmly between its teeth; little further skill was required for the swallowing of the contents. A native police officer stood by in the usual khaki uniform.

The actual grave took us a little by surprise. I had always thought in terms of a cave easy of access, with the body, 'bound hand and foot with grave clothes', laid to rest much after the style of the Garden Tomb in Jerusalem. But here it was necessary to descend a steep flight of awkward stairs, very roughly fashioned. At its foot, in the deep gloom which candlelight scarcely dissipated, was a further cavernous recess surmounted by a huge stone and only to be entered with difficulty. It was here, if this were indeed the tomb, that the mighty miracle took place. In the twinkling of an eye, as we must suppose and believe, the rottenness of death gave place to the full glow of physical health, so that when the bystanders removed the cerements of the tomb, Lazarus stood in their midst as palpable proof of the presence of One who was there and then RESUR-RECTION and LIFE. We almost forgot to look further at Bethany, its valley and its neighbouring hills, as we thought upon the unique happening of a day far removed from us in time, yet strangely present to the eye of faith. Still can we say:

> '*O strangely art Thou with us, Lord,*
> *Neither in height nor depth to seek;*
> *In nearness shall Thy voice be heard,*
> *Spirit to spirit Thou dost speak.*'

*

Leaving Bethany, and making the expected detour, we arrived shortly at Bethlehem. 'There was but a little way to come to Ephrath', as *Genesis* 35.16 quaintly expresses it [and Ephrath is Bethlehem], when we stopped by Rachel's tomb. It is supposed, probably rightly so, that the present massive memorial was erected several centuries ago by the Moslems, but it cannot be doubted that at this very spot, or in the near vicinity, as Jacob journeyed from Bethel southwards, Benjamin was born and Rachel died. Jacob set a pillar upon her grave [*Gen.* 35.20]. The present tomb fills most of the building which encloses it. The plastered walls bear, as do the walls of monuments in Britain, the names of those who, in the absence of a visitors' book, delight to leave visible evidence of their momentary presence in the place.

Robert Murray M'Cheyne's correspondence records the words: 'Returned by Bethlehem to Jerusalem. Bethlehem is a sweet village, placed on the top of a rocky hill – very white and dazzling. You see it on both sides of the hill. At Rachel's sepulchre you see Jerusalem on one hand and Bethlehem on the other, six miles apart'. It is just so, though perhaps the word 'sweet' would not normally spring to the lips. Across from the main road through the town – for town rather than village we must now call it – are the Shepherds' Fields. To my mind they were the pleasantest sight in the area. As one looked down upon them they seemed completely typical of the Palestinian scene, round-topped, receding into the distance, terraced and stony. It was easy to conjure up the picture of shepherds keeping watch over their flocks by night, and equally easy for one's inward ear to catch the lingering echoes of angelic song, giving glory to God and speaking blessing to men.

> *They speak to me of princely Tyre,*
> *That old Phoenician gem,*

Bethany, Bethlehem, Hebron, Petra

Great Sidon's daughter of the north;
But I will speak of Bethlehem.

'*They speak of Rome and Babylon –*
What can compare with them?
So let them praise their pride and pomp;
But I will speak of Bethlehem.

'*They speak of Athens, star of Greece,*
Her hill of Mars, her Academe,
Haunts of old wisdom and fair art;
But I will speak of Bethlehem.

'*Dear city, where heaven met with earth,*
Whence sprang the rod from Jesse's stem,
Where Jacob's star first shone – of these
I'll speak, O happy Bethlehem.'

HORATIUS BONAR

I confess that I could find no pleasure in our visit to the Church of the Nativity. Its garish interior seemed as far removed as ecclesiastical hands could render it from the natural simplicities of the setting for the actual birth. Certainly there was a manger, of marble; and in the centre of the floor of the building was a large ornamental star which, it was claimed, marked the precise spot where the birth took place. It may have been so – who can really say after this tremendous lapse of time? – but the complete absence of anything like reality in the surroundings robbed the place of all attractiveness as far as I was concerned. What I saw led me to remember the Crimean War as much as the birth of Christ, for it was a quarrel about the custodianship of this holy place which historians produce as one cause of that particular conflict between Russia and the West. But we sang a verse or two of 'Once in royal David's city' and endeavoured to bring our hearts into tune. In a recess of the building a couple of young ladies, pretty obviously attached to some near-by convent, knelt on the cool pavement, eyes apparently closed in adoration, almost as if carved in stone. Doubtless this served the purposes of ecclesiastical discipline, and at the same time was intended to symbolize, perhaps, the ceaseless watching of angels and archangels who 'thronged the holy birth'. It was very hard indeed to enter into the quiet magic of Phillips Brooks' lines:

> *'O little town of Bethlehem,*
> *How still we see thee lie!*
> *Above thy deep and dreamless sleep*
> *The silent stars go by:*
> *Yet in thy dark street shineth*
> *The everlasting Light;*
> *The hopes and fears of all the years*
> *Are met in thee tonight.*
>
> *For Christ is born of Mary;*
> *And, gathered all above,*
> *While mortals sleep, the angels keep*
> *Their watch of wondering love.'*

All was bustle and activity when we entered Bethlehem. Ours was a daytime visit, and buying and selling monopolized the attention of the throngs. We were shown a large workshop occupied by men skilled in their craft, who were carving olive-wood into elaborate figures and forms. From them we moved to premises next-door where their work was on sale. The more intricate pieces were wonderful products. From single fragments of wood, as I judged, they had carved, in one case, the figure of a shepherd carrying a lost and found sheep on his shoulder; in another, a shepherd resting with his flock under the shade of a tree, bringing to mind the ancient query, 'Tell me,

O thou whom my soul loveth, where thou . . . makest thy flock
to rest at noon'. The camel with its trappings was another
favourite subject of the wood-carvers, as also was David in
all the majesty of kingship. We looked and admired and at the
same time kept of necessity a tight control upon our purses.
Prices were high and, furthermore, the traveller must not over-
encumber himself. In any event, I was already making a collection of representative stones of the Land, one here, one
there. This was obviously cheaper, and it necessitated care in
gathering other ware, for the limits of weight for a 'plane trip
applied on the return as well as on the outward journey. It
was discreet therefore to resist the charms of olivewood and
of the artistry of the Bethlehem workmen.

It was a disappointment not to be taken to see the well of
Bethlehem 'which is by the gate', the more so as I had seen a
fairly recent photograph of it. Here, as a youth, David
must often have watered his flocks, and quenched his own
thirst.

> '*Oh for a draught of vintage! that hath been*
> *Cool'd a long age in the deep-delved earth.*'

For its water he greatly longed when three of his mighty men
broke through the ranks of the Philistines to win it, though,
because of impulses which can only be admired, he would not
drink it but poured it out unto the Lord [2 *Sam.* 23.14–17]. It
was good, however, to take a long look at the fields in which in
all probability he had tended his father's sheep, and where,
maybe, he had taken the lion by the beard and delivered a lamb
out of its mouth [1 *Sam.* 17.35]. Somewhere in the near neighbourhood also, we could imagine Naomi and her husband be-
moaning their troubles, setting out with their two sons for the
country of Moab, and the former returning in company with

Ruth but bereft of the rest. Somewhere in the landscape was the field which had belonged to Boaz, where he had instructed his men to let fall 'handfuls of purpose' so that Ruth the gleaner might experience at his hand the kindness of God. Bethlehem is, for the Bible lover, a veritable field of memory.

From outside the pages of Scripture, though closely linked with it, comes the remembrance that in Bethlehem, through the labours of Jerome, the Latin version of Scripture known as the Vulgate came to birth. A less pleasing thought reached us when our guide pointed to a hill in the distance known as The Mountain of the Franks, the reference being to the Crusaders who, it is said, here made their last stand against the Moslems. According to Josephus, the mound which stands somewhat curiously on the top of the hill was artificially made. It is the site of Herodion, one of Herod the Great's fortifications, and the king himself, adds the same historian, was buried here. It is remarkable that Herod should have been buried in this 'chosen palace-tomb' within sight of 'Bethlehem and all the coasts thereof' where his hatred for the infant Christ led to the death of 'the innocents'. It seems to belong to the ironies of history.

*

Our itinerary on this same occasion took us to Hebron which we reached by crossing the 'hill country of Judaea'. Again we looked upon hills terraced as we had seen them on the visit to Samaria, always of limestone and here and there planted with vines and olives. En route we paused at Solomon's Pools. It is not always safe to rely upon feelings. Some of us felt that to reach the Pools we had come down from Jerusalem, but here were pipes the purpose of which seemed to be to convey water from this spot to the city. Presumably therefore we were higher than Jerusalem, for there was no sign of arrangements for pumping the flow to higher levels. Whether the Pools can rightly be linked with Solomon is conjectural. We read in *Ecclesiastes* [2.6], 'I made me pools of water, to water there with the wood that bringeth forth trees', but it is another matter to conclude that these were the pools. The most that can be said is that the country between these Pools and Jerusalem has many evidences of waterworks and conduits artificially made. Traditionally they are linked with Solomon.

The territory which we now passed through is called in *2 Chronicles* 20.20 the 'wilderness of Tekoa'. It was by no means barren, however, although it lacked the fertility of better-watered areas. To it, in the time of David, Joab had sent to obtain the services of a wise woman – one would suppose her reputation to have been widespread – to assist him in his aim of bringing the exiled Absalom back to Jerusalem. At a later date it was the home country of Amos, the most outspoken of prophets, by occupation 'an herdman' and 'a gatherer of sycomore fruit' [*Amos* 1.1 and 7.14]. From the hills of Tekoa he had doubtless many times looked upon 'the seven stars and Orion', and seen 'the shadow of death turned into the morning,' by Him of whom it is said, 'The Lord is His Name' [*Amos* 5.8].

In due course we reached Hebron, over 3,000 feet above sea level, after travelling through a country where sheep and goats could, I surmise, find but a bare living. As we reached the city, which is altogether typical of the Land, there were signs of greatly increased fertility; vines, figs, olives and pomegranates were growing in profusion. It is more than likely that in this neighbourhood were the plains of Mamre, a name familiar to those who study the life of Abraham. Of all places in Palestine this is the one perhaps most closely associated with his name.

From a hill to the east of the city he is supposed to have looked towards the plain after the overthrow of Sodom and Gomorrah; we certainly know that from some vantage point in the area he saw the smoke from the doomed cities rising up to heaven like the smoke of a furnace [*Gen.* 19.28]. Later in the Bible story it was from the 'vale of Hebron' that Joseph, at the age of seventeen, went to Shechem, fifty miles to the north, and on to Dothan, to find his sheep-keeping brothers. Later still, Hebron became the inheritance of Caleb and a city of refuge. It became such a city to David in a different sense from that intended in *Joshua* 20. After the death of Saul he made special inquiry of God, 'Whither shall I go up?' The Lord answered him, 'Unto Hebron' [2 *Sam.* 2.1], and there, as king, he remained for seven and a half years [2 *Sam.* 5.5]. Sons were born to him there, including Absalom. In Hebron Abner was slain by Joab. Well might we take note of such a noted and notorious place!

We visited the Mosque in which, until fairly recently, no Christian [Nazarene] was allowed to set foot. Reputedly it is built over one of the most sacred spots in the Moslem world – the cave of Machpelah which Abraham bought from Ephron the Hittite for an agreed sum, 'current money with the merchant' [*Gen.* 23.16]. 'I will bury my dead there', were his mournful words. Removing our shoes as we entered, and noting the presence of worshippers engaged in silent devotions, we were allowed to peer, nothing more, through a small grating in the floor. Below, we were informed, were the tombs of Abraham and Sarah, Isaac and Rebecca, Jacob and Leah. Actually we could see nothing but a dim artificial light some distance down. Nearer to the tombs themselves we could not go. Alongside of us were worshippers of Allah touching the flagstones with their brows. To their left stood a time-piece, much after the pattern of a grandfather-clock. We had observed this same thing on the Dome of the Rock at Jerusalem. Its exact purpose we could only guess.

Also at Hebron we were taken to a decidedly ancient tree, railed off from our too close inspection, and called Abraham's oak. Under this tree, said our guide, Abraham entertained the three men who came to him as he sat in his tent door in the heat of the day, and informed him that his wife Sarah would bear him a son. He even added the detail that Sarah laughed when, from within the tent, she heard the news. Whether, as an Arab, he was dependent on the Koran, or was making reference to *Genesis* 18, I do not know, possibly the latter for he added that Sarah was seventy years old at the time, a mistake on his part for ninety; the Koran does not mention her age, but merely states that she and Abraham were old. We pondered with incredulous wonder the implication that the oak-tree was well-nigh four thousand years old, but kept our conclusions to ourselves. Acorns collected earlier from the tree were offered to all who cared to receive them. I helped myself to half a dozen to keep and hold them [unless I decide to raise oak-trees from some of them], together with aforementioned stones, as mementoes of the Land and of our day of visitation. I had already collected stones from the middle of Hezekiah's tunnel and from the Garden Tomb, and was shortly to obtain more from Petra, the Dead Sea, Jericho, Wadi Musa, Hazor, Galilee, Megiddo, and other spots, not for the sake of geological but of historical interest, and maybe for sentiment too.

*

Petra, we decided, was worth a visit, though, as the mileage was very considerable, the outward and return journeys together occupying a long day, not all members of our party made the trip. We left Jerusalem shortly after dawn, took the road that led to the Dead Sea, by-passed Jericho, crossed the Jordan by the Allenby Bridge, as if making for Amman, but shortly forked right, turned south, and were soon running parallel to the Dead Sea on its eastern side. We were heading for the King's Highway, noted of old [*Num.* 20.19; *Deut.* 2.27]. To the west we passed Mount Nebo, memorable as the place from which Moses viewed the Land which he was forbidden to enter, and the nameless vale where God Himself saw to the obsequies of His servant:

> '*By Nebo's lonely mountain,*
> *On this side Jordan's wave,*
> *In a vale in the land of Moab*
> *There lies a lonely grave;*
> *And no man knows that sepulchre,*
> *And no man saw it e'er,*
> *For the angels of God upturn'd the sod*
> *And laid the dead man there.*
>
> '*Perchance the bald old eagle*
> *On grey Beth-Peor's height,*
> *Out of his lonely eyrie*
> *Look'd on the wondrous sight;*
> *Perchance the lion, stalking,*
> *Still shuns the hallow'd spot,*
> *For beast and bird have seen and heard*
> *That which man knoweth not.*
>
> '*O lonely grave in Moab's land,*
> *O dark Beth-Peor's hill!*
> *Speak to these curious hearts of ours*
> *And teach them to be still:*
> *God hath His mysteries of grace,*
> *Ways that we cannot tell;*

He hides them deep, like the hidden sleep
Of him He loved so well.'

C. FRANCES ALEXANDER

We were, in fact, now in ancient Moab, and proceeding with all speed to Edom on an excellent road which seemed made for the tourist. For some distance the country was fertile and undulating. At frequent intervals we passed camels in varying numbers; one particular train seemed to contain fifty or sixty of them. The black tents of the Bedouin, either singly or in small clusters, were the only indication of human habitation. In an hour or two the hills had given place to a stony or sandy terrain, normally level, with little vegetation to encourage animal life. Birds of any kind we very rarely saw.

After a time we called at Sahara Rest, where refreshments were procurable and where heated car engines could obtain a brief repose. Pressing onwards as we could, we passed out of Moab into Edom, Esau's country, described by the famous traveller, Charles M. Doughty, in his *Arabia Deserta* as 'a great barrenness of gravel stones' [1.68]. We could easily concur with his verdict. Soon we were approaching Maan, and reached Wadi Musa, Moses's Valley, where we found fresh cool running water. Here, we were informed, was where Moses struck the rock and the waters gushed out. Was the reference to the second occasion of such a happening, we wondered: it could not possibly refer to the first, for that took place in the Sinai region, many miles distant.

It was not long before we reached the Petra area, having passed through a district of limestone, downs and combes, which, says Doughty, are 'like the country about Bath'. I can neither contradict nor confirm the assertion but Doughty's fame inclines me to receive it as truth.

We had now reached the flat plain immediately in front of

The Syk [pronounced Seek], the narrow winding passage through the mountains which is the only really practicable route to Petra, the 'rose-red city half as old as Time', as J. W. Burgon described it. Its walls are precipitous, of various colours, and occupied, where roothold is obtainable, by the wild fig. Oleanders abound in the neighbourhood. The cars could proceed no further, but at this point horses were available and a cavalcade was soon in progress. In tribute to the Jordanian government I may here remark that toilets of the European type – those at the Sahara Rest were anything but agreeable to Europeans – had been constructed at government expense for the benefit of tourists. An Arab who thought to make illicit gain by demanding one shilling per head for their use by our party was severely reprimanded by a member of the uniformed police who happened to be at the spot at the time of our arrival and became acquainted with the offence. Some of us preferred to walk through the Syk in the hope of observing more than was possible on horseback and of obtaining the exercise denied to us by a long car journey. Underfoot were loose pebbles and we could well imagine surging torrents tearing through the passage when a storm burst over the district. We learned to our surprise that, not more than three or four weeks previously, there had been a heavy fall of snow. To us it seemed as if high summer held perpetual sway. Snow and Petra seemed incompatibles.

We had not walked more than a couple of miles at most before our guide announced that he proposed to conduct us off the beaten track to a high place of ancient sacrifice only to be reached by a fairly arduous climb. We accomplished it with zest and not inconsiderable pleasure. We saw the land of Edom at its wildest, for it was difficult to conceive of anything wilder and more awesome than the type of country which we now entered. Not that it was a climb worthy of a mountaineer; my meaning merely is that it was rocky and tortuous, that it occasionally involved the use of hands as well as feet, and that it was easy to miss the way. Steps had been cut here and there in the more difficult ascents. Lizards [or were they chameleons?] darted brightly among the stones and hid in the crevices of the rocks. We sometimes stopped to watch their comings and goings. Blues and yellows predominated. A flat surface of vertical rock occasionally displayed carvings which appeared to be centuries, if not millenniums, old. At one point our attention was called to lettering which had defied decipherment and understanding. Ultimately, in the top of the hills, we reached the place of sacrifice. A shallow rectangular pit had been hewn out in the rock, and an altar of rock left at its centre. At one side was the channel by which the blood of the victims had been drained away. It was awesome to stand at the place and look around at the tangle of mountains and vales which stretched as far as eye could see. While we looked and wondered the guide asked us to follow his finger as he pointed to a peak in the near distance. 'That', he explained, 'is Mount Hor, the place where Aaron died'. The news took us aback for, despite our sight of the water from the rock at Wadi Musa, we had hardly realized that we were standing on the borders of the wild and dismal country once traversed by the people of Israel as they were led by the 'fiery cloudy pillar' from Egypt to the Promised Land. But in fact our journey that very day had been, in reverse, along the route followed by Israel so that they might enter the Land, not by way of Beersheba and Hebron, but by way of the Jordan Valley and Jericho.

Horatius Bonar has a very striking poem entitled 'Mount Hor', in which he describes the scenery of the country on which we were now looking:

'They come not to gaze on the matchless glory,
On grandeur the like of which earth has not –
A billowy ocean of mountains hoary,
A chaos of cliffs round this awful spot;
A vision like that in some old-world story,
Too terrible ever to be forgot.

'The desert rainbow that gleams before ye,
But leaves your solitude doubly bleak;
The shadows of sunset fall ghastly o'er ye;
Cliff frowns upon cliff, and peak on peak:
O rocks of the desolate, lean and hoary,
What lip of man can your grandeur speak!

'Splintered and blasted and thunder-smitten,
Not a smile above, nor a hope below;
Shivered and scorched and hunger-bitten,
No earthly lightning has seamed your brow:
On each stone the Avenger's pen has written
Horror and ruin and death and woe.'

But now it was time for us to descend from the heights, and
after passing numerous caves of differing shapes and sizes we
reached the circular plateau surrounded by the hills of red rock
for which Petra is famous. It is a singular coincidence that the
prevailing colour of Edom's capital should be RED, since
Edom and Esau alike mean 'red'. The whole area, though now
a picture of desolation [the tourist traffic apart] seems in its
palmy days to have been a mart of nations. Despite its geographical setting, far from the sea and from the East's capital
cities, it was so placed as to become a rendez-vous for camel
caravans. When merchants crossed Arabia from the Persian
Gulf it was here that they first touched on the civilized world.
Petra thus became a depot for goods of exchange. The traffic

that converged upon it from the East branched from it again to Egypt, Palestine, and Syria by a variety of routes.

The Hebrew prophets have much to say about Edom, including Petra. 'Edom shall be a desolation', says *Jeremiah* [49.17], 'perpetual desolations' says *Ezekiel* [35.3, 9]. 'Thy terribleness hath deceived thee, and the pride of thine heart, O thou that dwellest in the clefts of the rock' – as did Petra's inhabitants – 'that holdest the height of the hill; though thou shouldest make thy nest as high as the eagle, I will bring thee down from thence, saith the Lord' [*Jer.* 49.16]. Even David has a word to bequeath to us about the place: 'Who will bring me into the strong city? Who will lead me into Edom?' [*Ps.* 108.10].

It has been estimated that, in ancient days, Petra supported a population of as many as 30,000. Its buildings, cut out of the solid rock, could only have resulted from the labours of many. Not far from the 'city centre' is a Roman amphitheatre [for the Roman Empire reached as far as this] capable of seating about 3,000 spectators. It contained 33 rows of seats cut out of the rock. In front of it ran a paved way which was unmistakably Roman in construction. From Hadrian's Wall to Petra the Romans have most certainly left their monumental marks.

Our Tourist Agency had arranged for those of our party who availed themselves of this optional excursion to have a meal in Petra's only hotel; the only surprise was that there should exist such a building in such an outlandish spot. I found myself sitting alongside a young man from Leeds who was intently examining a reference to Edom in the prophecy of Obadiah: 'Though thou exalt thyself as the eagle, and though thou set thy nest among the stars, thence will I bring thee down, saith the Lord' [v. 4]. Another evidence that the Word of God is still the best guide book to the Holy Land and its near neighbours!

It was now time to return to the waiting cars at the entrance to The Syk. As we did so we investigated the dark interiors of several of Petra's temples, and tested their powers to echo the human voice. The sheer labour involved in their construction baffles the imagination. Surmounting the entrance to one of the largest of them is a huge stone urn which bears signs of bullet marks. We were told that Arabs were responsible for the shooting, to test their theory that the urn contained treasure. To all appearances the urn was solid.

The weariness of the return journey through the Syk was countered by conversation. Discussion turned upon matters prophetic, matters doctrinal, and even upon the merits of '*The Genesis Flood*' as explained and expounded by Messrs. Morris and Whitcomb. Once aboard our cars we settled down to a period of comparative silence. The cars were speedy and the road from start to finish remarkably good, yet the return journey seemed twice as long as that of the morning. Distance, like time, can be long or short according to the state of one's mind, the degree of interest of a subject, and the measure of tiredness of the human body.

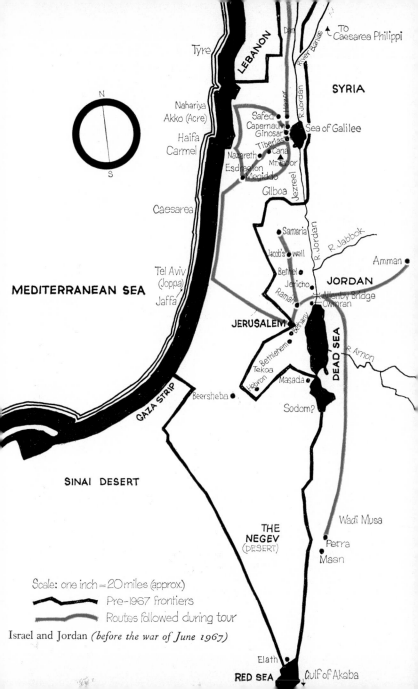

N

TO
Caesarea Philippi

Tyre

LEBANON

Dan

River Banias

SYRIA

R. Jordan

Hazor

Nahariya
Akko (Acre)

Safed
Capernaum
Ginosar

Sea of Galilee

Haifa
Carmel

Tiberias

Nazareth
Cana
Mt. Tabor

Esdraelon
Megiddo

Jezreel

Gilboa

Caesarea

Samaria

R. Jordan

R. Jabbok

Jacob's well

Bethel

Amman

Tel Aviv
(Joppa)

Jericho

JORDAN

Jaffa

Ramah

Allenby Bridge
Qumran

MEDITERRANEAN SEA

JERUSALEM

Bethany

Bethlehem

DEAD SEA

R. Arnon

Tekoa

Hebron

Masada

Beersheba

Sodom?

GAZA STRIP

SINAI DESERT

Wadi Musa

THE
NEGEV
(DESERT)

Petra
Maan

Scale: one inch = 20 miles (approx.)

Pre-1967 frontiers

Routes followed during tour

Israel and Jordan (*before the war of June 1967*)

Elath

RED SEA Gulf of Akaba

The Old City of Jerusalem as seen from the Mount of Olives.

Jerusalem: The Wailing Wall before the war of June, 1967. This is reputed to be all that survives of Herod's temple. Through the Christian era it has been a spot where Jews bewailed the destruction of the city and temple in A.D. 70. See page 139

(*above*) Jerusalem: The
Wailing Wall since June,
1967. Shortly after its
capture by Israel, property
which concealed it from
view and hindered
access to it was destroyed.

(*below*) Siloam (or
Hezekiah's) Tunnel. This
was constructed by King
Hezekiah about 701 B.C.
to divert the water of
Gihon inside Jerusalem
and deprive the invading
Assyrians of its use. See
pages 56–58, 65–67.

(*above*) The Garden Tomb. This is close to the Damascus Gate and near to Gordon's Calvary. See pages 70–73.

(*below*) Golgotha as identified by General Gordon. It is near the Damascus Gate. See pages 70–71.

(*above*) Bethlehem, The City of David. A general view. See pages 98–102.

(*below*) Tel Aviv with Jaffa (Joppa) in the background. Ancient and modern are united in the present city, the largest in the land with a population of 600,000. See page 152.

Rachel's Tomb, Bethlehem. See page 98.

Hebron: market scene. Hebron was David's capital city before the capture of Jerusalem. See pages 103–105.

Beersheba: Market day.

(*above*) Masada: site of Herod's fortress on the western side of the Dead Sea. This was captured by the Romans in A.D. 73. The Roman ramp is plainly visible. See pages 139–48.

(*below*) Masada: Synagogue. This is the remains of Israel's earliest known synagogue— built in the days of Herod, captured and used by the Romans as a stable, captured and rebuilt by the Zealots, finally recaptured and destroyed by the Romans.

Nazareth: a street scene.

The Twelve Tribes as commemorated in Israeli postage stamps.
Row 1: Reuben, Simeon, Levi. Row 2: Judah, Dan, Naphtali. Row 3: Gad,
Asher, Issachar. Row 4: Zebulun, Joseph, Benjamin. The symbolism is based
upon the blessing of the tribes as found in Genesis 49 and Deuteronomy 33.

THE JORDAN

Come with me to Jordan's stream,
  Friend and brother of my soul,
Where the aspen's fresh leaves gleam,
  Where the rapid waters roll.

From yon desert Israel's host,
  [God a wondrous path bestowing],
Dry-shod thro' these waters crossed,
  Jordan all his banks o'erflowing.

Israel's noblest prophets there
  Passed between the waters riven;
One a fiery chariot bare
  By a whirlwind up to heaven.

Hither came th' Eternal Son,
  Ere the tempter's wiles were tried;
Him did God the Father own
  From the heavens opening wide.

There the Spirit like a dove,
  Plenteously on Him was poured:
Henceforth let that Spirit's love
  Bind our hearts in sweet accord.

H. B. WHITAKER CHURTON

So far as our stay in the Land of Jordan is concerned, it remains to describe the visit we paid to the lower Jordan Valley. By means of it we made acquaintance with Jericho, the Dead Sea, and the district where the Dead Sea scrolls were discovered in recent years. Our journey led us, as before, down the Jericho road, now a first-class road for motorcars. Some of the chief awkwardnesses of the ancient highway have of late years been eliminated. As in so many other matters the traveller by motor cannot even faintly appreciate the difference between ancient and modern times unless he has been favoured with some knowledge of Scripture or, otherwise, of travel in olden times.

Jericho is approximately twenty miles from Jerusalem by an almost continual descent. No cyclist would speak well of the uphill journey, though the descent would be glorious. For most of the way the hills are too barren to support life, though possibly the hardiest of goats might here and there contrive to survive. Mid-way between the two cities we stopped at the Good Samaritan Inn, where it was not difficult to call to mind the appropriate parable, and the Lord's delightful answer to the question, 'And who is my neighbour?'. One could well imagine that none but travellers who found themselves benighted or under some other form of compulsion would ever wish to break their journey in so desolate a spot. But the courtyard was commodious and capable of accommodating many camels. It was built around a well which had most certainly determined its precise location. We did not loiter [though one member of the party chose to canter around on horseback], but continued our plunge downward to the spot which is acclaimed by every traveller to be the lowest part of the earth's crust which remains dry land. Even so, when the Dead Sea is reached, the declivity continues under the sea-bed to a further depth of 1300 feet. The great rift valley down which the Jordan flows, and which commences near the Lebanon mountains, continues to the Gulf of Akaba and far beyond into Africa. Between the southern end of the Dead Sea and the Gulf it is crossed by a ridge of hills. Had this not been so it is more than likely that the Red Sea would have reached up as far as Galilee with tremendous results for many nations. God's hand has directed otherwise, however. The Dead Sea is of His making. It is the watery grave of the cities of the plain after they had been deluged by fire. 'The Lord rained upon Sodom and Gomorrah brimstone and fire from the Lord out of heaven'. [*Gen.* 19.24]. Peter describes it as 'condemnation with an overthrow' [2 *Pet.* 2.6]. It was so complete that the archaeologist cannot tell with any certainty whether the cities are beneath the Sea, to the south of it or to the north of it. Phineas Fletcher, a minor poet of the seventeenth century, describes the Dead Sea as

> *'that dreadful lake —*
> *No turning path, or issue thence is found:*
> *Hell's self is pictured in that brimstone wave'.*

Type it is of the lake of fire and brimstone which is the second death.

The great difference in height between Jerusalem 'in the top of the mountains' and Jericho in the low-lying valley accounts for the change in climate which cannot but be felt by the man who goes down from the one to the other. Jerusalem has its olives, Jericho is 'the city of palm trees' [*Deut.* 34.3]. The capital city enjoys mountain air, the tropical city induces a feeling of breathlessness in the visitor. He is liable, especially in the heat of the summer, when the temperature may rise to as much as 130 degrees in the shade, to lose all vigour and vitality during his stay. Our visit, however, took place before the extreme of heat set in, and the thermometer during our brief stay did not register more than perhaps 80 or 85 degrees Fahrenheit.

*

Modern Jericho has been rendered habitable from ancient days by the presence of perennial springs, the chief of which is Elisha's fountain, yielding 1000 gallons a minute with but little variation; we entered it shortly after we reached Dead Sea level. It is a pleasant little place, with a wealth of tropical or sub-tropical vegetation, and valued as a winter resort by the better-class citizens of Jerusalem. Our interest, however, was concentrated on the 'tell' [mound] of ancient Jericho, situated a little way beyond the modern town. It has been the scene of intensive exploration for decades past.

Interest in the 'tell' began in 1867 when the Palestine Exploration Fund, a British Society [founded two years earlier] undertook the first modern investigation of the place. No great progress was then made. An Austro-German expedition went over the same ground about 1910, but again without any remarkable results. About 1930, Professor John Garstang of

Liverpool University recommenced digging, and shortly the Christian world was informed that his discoveries confirmed the biblical account of the capture of Jericho by Joshua in several particulars. In addition it was claimed that the professor had virtually solved a much-disputed problem, namely, the date of the Exodus from Egypt under Moses. He had done this, it was urged, by discovering the ancient necropolis [cemetery] of Jericho, finding in it scarabs [almost like modern brooches] imported from Egypt and bearing the cartouches [hieroglyphics within oval rings] of certain Pharaohs whose dates were known from Egyptian chronology, and deducing from such evidence the date when, the city being destroyed by Joshua and rendered a desolation, burials in the necropolis ceased. The latest scarab, therefore, would fix within narrow limits the date of destruction. The evidence appeared to indicate a date for the Exodus of about 1440 BC, as against a date around 1280 BC favoured by many scholars.

In the nineteen-fifties another and even more thorough series of excavations at Jericho was undertaken by Dr Kathleen Kenyon on behalf of the British School of Archaeology in Jerusalem. She came to the conclusion that, amid the welter of ancient settlements, some of them walled, which had occupied the site during its tremendously long history, Professor Garstang had made sundry miscalculations and unjustified deductions. The successive towns and their walls had been destroyed at various widely-separated times, said Dr Kenyon, so that it was all too easy to adopt incorrect identifications. The consequence was that the date of the Exodus again became a matter of argument between archaeological experts. Even so, it is correct to say that Jericho has been one of the most interesting and rewarding of sites in the Holy Land.

We stood upon the much-excavated mound, which is all

that is to be seen of the ancient city, with mixed feelings. It was in the middle of the seventeenth century, apparently, that the unpleasant expletive, 'Go to Jericho', or 'You may go to Jericho for all I care' came into popular use. But far from this having befallen us in any evil sense, here we were at Jericho from the most desirable of motives, and determined to make the most of the opportunity.

As a matter of fact there was not a great deal to be seen on the mound itself. It was much after the style of a pit heap in industrial England or Wales where worthless slag has accumulated, though perhaps it was much less regular in shape. But there was one marked difference which came to mind. No one lives or has lived on a slag heap, but we had the sure knowledge that the dust and stones on which our feet were at that moment planted represented millenniums of human settlement, and were in fact as historic as almost any other spot on earth. Dr Kenyon seems inclined to regard Jericho as the world's oldest city, a city very old indeed when the cities of Europe were yet unborn. We enter into no disputation on this matter, but can well believe that no city east or west of Palestine is able to produce evidence of greater antiquity. When Rome was a hamlet and London a morass, the city of palm trees had doubtless been a flourishing centre of culture for years out of mind.

The knowledge that one was standing on such a historic mound produced a thrill second only to that which resulted from the unyielding testimony of Holy Scripture. Outside Scripture one is swayed this way or that way by the rival conjectural inferences of the experts in archaeology. When Scripture speaks, the mind rests on authoritative utterance. And so we took stock of the scene with the sacred text in mind. We were standing within the confines of the most famous valley on earth, somewhat amazed by its width and general amplitude. It glared white in the heat which poured down upon it from a cloudless sky. To the East rose the long mountain wall which we know as the mountains of Gilead and Moab. Westwards were the mountains of Judaea, broken up by countless transverse valleys and reaching their peak in the city of God. The historic Jordan flowed down the centre of the valley, unseen from Jericho but of immense value to its site.

Imagination, fired and fed by Scripture, could readily take in the ancient situation. A host consisting of an entire nation – men, women and children, not to say sucklings also [out of whose mouths the Lord has perfected praise] – had arrived from the south after skirting Moab. The word had spread to city and plain that they 'covered the face of the earth', and were about 'to lick up all that are round about . . . as the ox licketh up the grass of the field' [*Num.* 22.4, 11]. Moab had introduced the soothsayer of the East to bring a curse upon them, but the curse had been turned into a blessing, and he could not reverse it. Certainly the Israelitish leader had died, but the advance had continued. What could Jericho do to meet the emergency and the peril?

On its part Israel lived in hope. God had buried His workman, but was carrying on His work. Joshua had succeeded Moses. Jordan was within sight, its bed greatly extended by the melting of the snows of Hermon. Possibly it was a mile or more in width. 'The Captain of Israel's host and Guide' was present lest they should miss their 'providential way',

> *'As far from danger as from fear,*
> *While Love, almighty Love, was near.'*

Jericho was devoted to destruction, according to the word of the Lord. Its walls were to fall down flat with the exception of a house occupied by one particular family; its inhabitants must perish in the fall of the city. God's decree had gone out against them. And God's people did not shrink from the awful issues. Certain meaningful ceremonial must accompany the tragic event.

All this and more it was not difficult for the mind's eye to see happening as we stood for a while on the 'tell'. We could not descend to the depth of the excavations for these were defended by barbed-wire defences. We heard that this had but recently been placed in position, following on an untoward event in which visitors were involved. We could, however, look down on the exposed walls from above and conjecture which of them represented the city of Joshua's day. The degree of desolation which everywhere met the eye graphically portrayed the completeness with which the Israelites accomplished their task. The mound of Jericho now belongs to 'the perpetual desolations' which occur quite plentifully in the Near East. No trace of the twelve stones which Israel placed on the western bank of the Jordan in commemoration of the crossing, or of the twelve stones placed in the bed of the river now remains, but, as elsewhere, I made my own selection of a small Jericho stone, and with its companions it lies close at my hand bearing its silent witness to the events linked with its place of origin. Others may fill their bottles with Jordan water; for myself I prefer twelve [or more] stones chosen from various parts of the Land.

Behind Jericho, on its western side, was the mountain traditionally associated with the temptation of the Lord in the wilderness. We were unable to visit it, but we took note of its position, and urged memory to take its flight over fourteen hundred years of time and to take us in thought from Joshua of Jericho fame to One who bore the same Name and who was tempted in all points like as we are, yet without sin [*Heb*. 4.15].

*

Soon we moved on to the Jordan River and were quickly occupied in bathing our feet in its cooling waters, regretful only that we lacked opportunity to explore its course from its outlet into the Dead Sea to its source at the base of Hermon. But it was our privilege later to set eyes on its upper waters. Geographers, skilfully distinguishing region from region, delight to tell us that the Jordan takes its rise under the shadow of the heights of Lebanon, flows through Lake Huleh, [now no more, for it has been drained in recent months], enters and flows through the Sea of Galilee, and then flows down for another 65 miles [during which it meanders for some 200 miles] to the sweltering heat of the Dead Sea from which there is no outlet. Philip Henry Gosse, in an old work [1850] entitled '*Sacred Streams*' wrote:

> *The Jordan – a river absolutely unique in the whole world; cleft in the very bowels of the earth; being, at its issue from the Lake of Galilee, far below the sea-level, and ever plunging lower and lower, by twenty-seven distinct descents, till it empties into the Dead Sea, that horrid yawning chasm of salt and pitch and desolation, whose surface is actually 1,300 feet below the Mediterranean, the awful grave of those cities "set forth for an example, suffering the vengeance of eternal fire" [Jude 7]. Throughout the Scripture this wondrous river stands as the type of penal death, and may we not say, of death issuing in hell? Its very name is significant, whether we accept the etymology which reads "the Descender", or that, which seems the better one, of "the River of Judgment" [Jor = River, and Dan = Judgment]*

The Jordan is connected in Holy Scripture with some of the most interesting events of all time – the overthrow of the Cities of the Plain, as renowned for the mode of their destruction as for their wickedness; the entry of Israel into the Land of Promise when the river was 'driven back'; the translation of

Elijah; the recovery of a borrowed axe-head, when 'the iron did swim'; the healing of a soldier who, only a brief time previously, had 'turned and gone away in a rage', scorning the counsel of the prophet; the ministry of a prophet than whom there was none greater among those born of women; and the baptism of the Lord Jesus as He came forth to fulfil all righteousness. Much there is, in very truth, to stir the memory as the Jordan comes in sight. In itself it is by no means an impressive river, any more than certain villages and towns in the Land are in the least degree impressive for size or grandeur. But considered historically and as a factor in sacred story, it is a greater river by far than waters of vastly greater dimensions. The principle contained in the warning, 'Look not on the height of his stature' applies to man's environment as well as to his person.

*

From Jordan we moved on to the Dead Sea. It was 'toward evening and the day was far spent'. In consequence it was not altogether possible to find agreement with travellers who depict the area as a fearful example of desolation and dereliction. Dr Kenyon, in her '*Digging up Jericho*', goes so far as to say of the Mountains of Gilead and Moab and the eastern side of the Jordan Valley that 'when the setting sun shines on these hills, they take on an appearance of incredible loveliness, in shades of blue and mauve which are never the same'. She is speaking of the view opposite Jericho, but her words are not inapplicable to the eastern shores of the Dead Sea also. The area appears less desolate than formerly, as of late years a hotel has been erected at the northern end of the Sea, and there are arrangements for bathing. The waters are most certainly saline, intensely so, as the slightest taste of them indicates, and swimming is an art easily practised. Various members of our party braved the pebbly shore to reach the small jetty where bathing is carried on, and to acquire the necessary qualification for boasting of immersion in the salty solution, but I confess that I was glad to emerge after a brief experience in the shallows. The pebbles both on the shore and beneath the waters were indeed painful. My resolution to keep my head above water was partly successful, and a little salt in the eye was soon washed away by nature's own remedy.

Close to the Dead Sea is Cwmran, the site of the monastery of the sect of the Essenes which has been excavated quite recently. In its near neighbourhood are the caves in which the famous biblical and other scrolls were found, to the vast amazement of scholars from 1948 onwards. It was all but incredible that scrolls which took the text of Scripture back a thousand years should be discovered in such an unpromising area. By a miracle of preservation the scrolls have vindicated the text of the Word as we have received it.

Some members of our party who had spied out the spot two years previously had reported that it was of but small visual interest, but undeterred by their 'evil report', several of us decided to seek it out. The remains are certainly not impressive and the caves are not approachable by the unskilled scrambler, but the visit was memorable. Little beyond a few foundations was to be seen in the sandy elevated waste, merely a few low walls of stone, arranged in small squares and rectangles. One had to take it on trust that here had been a monastery inhabited by a zealous community which had spurned city life and sought to work out its own brand of righteousness in scenes far removed from the busy haunts of men. During our brief stay the only living creatures we encountered were the sand flies which welcomed the unanticipated occasion by selecting at least one lady member of the party as their legitimate prey.

It would have been of no small interest to sail on the waters of this lifeless Sea. But even had there been a boat to convey us, it would have been impracticable, for down the centre of the Sea from north to south runs the frontier between Jordan and Israel, and who can say precisely where it is to be discerned? The Sea of Galilee presents no such difficulty for it lies entirely within the State of Israel.

Again I quote from *Sacred Streams*:

> *The bottom of the Sea consists of two submerged plains, an elevated and a depressed one. The former is the roundish bay which forms the southern extremity, separated from the rest of the sea by a promontory which runs nearly all the way across; the bottom in this part is pretty evenly about twelve or fifteen feet below the surface . . . The other area, the great body of the sea, has a nearly uniform depth of a thousand feet: while, through its centre, in a line corresponding with the course of the Jordan, there runs a ravine, cleaving the bottom to the depth of two hundred feet more.*
>
> *The inference then is obvious, that once, this level area formed the beauteous and fertile plain of Sodom, well watered everywhere by the Jordan [and probably many affluent streams], whose flood was poured along the ravine or deep bed running through it; and that the whole plain, after having its bituminous crust devoured by "fire and brimstone out of heaven", was made to sink down suddenly a thousand feet, not in fragments, but in a mass, with the river-bed still cutting it, as an indelible memorial of the truth of the Word of God. The great and deep gulf thus formed then constituted a reservoir, into which the Jordan's waters gradually poured, until they attained the level which they now possess.*

Geologists, geographers and others have reached no agreement on such matters as these, but the relationship of geography and Scripture in this case is of particular interest, and we cannot forget that Old Testament and New Testament alike present the Christian with statements on the spiritual significance of events in the region of the Dead Sea. Amazingly we read in Ezekiel of the restoration of life to the Dead Sea; the prophet speaks of it as a 'healing' [47.8], and for good measure adds that fishers will in that day stand on the east and west shores of the Sea and net fish of all kinds, 'as the fish of the great sea [i.e. the Mediterranean], exceeding many'. Read and interpret such statements as we may, they certainly invite consideration, and the traveller in the Land does well to call them to mind.

In the New Testament it is the Lord Himself who bids us 'remember Lot's wife'. Regrettably it was not possible for us to reach the locality to the south of the Sea where stands the 'pillar of salt' still described by the Arabs as Lot's wife. We must therefore quote again from one of several possible descriptions. Our choice falls upon that given by an American, Lieutenant Lynch, who in 1848 made extensive explorations in the Jordan Valley. He was in command of an expedition fitted out at the expense of the United States government, and sailed from Galilee to the Dead Sea with two metallic boats, one of copper and one of iron, which had been transported with great labour from the Mediterranean Sea to the Sea of Galilee. In connection with Lot's wife he wrote thus:

We saw, to our great astonishment, on the eastern side of Usdum [Sodom], a lofty round pillar, standing apparently detached from the general mass, at the head of a deep, narrow, and abrupt chasm. We immediately pulled in for the shore and examined it. We found it to be of solid salt, capped with carbonate of lime, cylindrical in front and pyramidical behind. The upper or rounded part is about forty feet high, resting on a kind of oval pedestal, from forty to sixty feet above the level of the sea. It slightly decreases in size upward, crumbles at the top, and is one entire mass of crystallization.

Similar pillars in the area have, by different travellers, been described as Lot's wife; in fact it is clear that the entire locality is a permanent memorial to the divine act of judgment which was intended to demonstrate to later generations 'the vengeance of eternal fire' [*Jude* v.7].

*

As viewed by a person in the region of the Dead Sea, sunlight begins to fade comparatively early in the day. The fiery glow of sunset illuminates the crests of the Judaean hills and shadows lengthen almost before the citizens of Jerusalem have begun to realize that the sun has passed its zenith. Our afternoon passed all too quickly, even though certain of our fellow-tourists complained of the heat and of the feeling of lassitude which accompanied it. Once aboard our cars, the twenty-mile-long gradient was soon traversed and we were back in the comforts of our hotel on Olivet. As I conclude this [Jordanian] part of my narrative I cannot but point the contrast between the ease and luxury which wait on the modern tourist and the discomforts inseparable from eastern travel as late as the nineteenth century. The refinements of a hotel of the nineteen-sixties, whether in Europe or in the Near East, need not here by outlined. At the other extreme I illustrate the trials of the traveller by an extract chosen from John Gadsby's *My Wanderings* – his travels in the East at various dates between 1846 and 1853. The spot described is Jericho.

> *Of all the miserable places I have ever beheld, this village is the most miserable. The cottages are merely mud walls, with dried leaves and branches of trees for roofs. These were intended only to keep out the sun, for a heavy shower of rain would*

speedily sweep through the whole. There are no windows nor any doorways except a hole about as large as the entrance to a decent-sized pigsty. No Irish mud cabin that I have ever seen was half so wretched. And had we to take up our temporary abode in one of these? Yes! for our "Christian" guide had told us our tent would be unnecessary, as we should have good lodgings; therefore we had disposed of it. "And which," said I, "is to be our happy home?" "Dat," replied Abdullah, pointing to one just before us. I looked and saw a woman beating out a donkey, and then a goat, after which she bustled about and began to sweep out the dirt which the donkey and goat had left. Then she looked [for she was unveiled] as if she had performed some extraordinary exploit. And then I laughed. And then she looked wonderfully pleased, and retired, calling out "Tyeeb, Tyeeb!" ["Good, good!"], doubtless imagining that I was as pleased as she was. But she was wrong, for it struck me as being somewhat cruel to turn a couple of quadrupeds out of their quarters to make room for bipeds, and no less cruel for the bipeds to be compelled to occupy their places.

The poor woman, we found, might have done her work better, as she had left in the place a large quantity of decayed rubbish, which the animals had refused to eat and had trampled under foot. I was soon convinced that there was no sleep for me. Abdullah brushed round a square place on the mud floor, and then spread my quilt and placed my carpet bag for a pillow, which looked comfortable enough; and I felt my heart drawn out in gratitude to God for His mercies to me. But the vermin was beyond all endurance. Mr T. [Gadsby's companion] rolled about and slept on; fatigue had mastered him for the time being. I threw myself down, and doubling myself up, covered my whole body, head and all, with my rug, for cockroaches, crickets, and other creeping things were continually dropping from the leaves which formed the roof. And as for fleas, there is nothing in all Egypt to equal them. The frogs in the marshes were croaking by thousands; and all sorts of noises except the barking of dogs prevailed throughout the night. There was not a single dog in the village, as there was nothing there on which dogs could live, and yet human beings were eking out their miserable existence. . . . I would recommend any one who wishes to learn early rising to go to Jericho. I counted no less than 150 punctures on one wrist, and my whole body was in the same state; for the fleas in the east always bite through my skin, and leave a mark as if pierced with an awl.

Gadsby adds that the women of Jericho were as repellent in appearance as the accommodation they offered was uncongenial to sleep. 'Their lips', he wrote, 'were all dyed blue and their chins tattooed. I greatly wished they had been veiled, like the Egyptians, for they looked pitiable objects.'

Let the modern tourist be correspondingly thankful!

MASADA

The King of Judaea was crafty and wise,
But not with the wisdom that comes from the skies.
His nest on the crag he most artfully reared,
And was safe from the foes which aforetime he feared.

His stores were filled plenty with all kinds of foods;
His palace reflected his various moods;
And cisterns he dug that he might take his fill
Of the torrents so rare when they fell on the hill.

But the time came when Herod was summoned away
To meet his Creator and attend judgment-day;
'Twas after his anger 'gainst Eastern wise men,
And his slaughter of infants in far Bethlehem.

Masada then passed to the armies of Rome,
But was captured by Zealots who made it their home;
And when Salem was captured by Titus's men,
It resisted them boldly again and again.

But Rome, all determined to quicken the pace,
Constructed a ramp up strong Masada's face;
She circled the Zealots around by a wall,
And thus hastened the day when the fortress must fall.

The climax was fearful; the beleaguered Jews
Felt they could not escape and 'twere better to lose
At their own hands their lives, and ward off the disgrace;
So they cheated the Romans and ended their race.

The stones of Masada, explored by the hand
Of Salem's own children, restored to the Land,
Tell the story of valour, with detail all new,
'Tis known now to millions instead of the few.

And Israel's children, a numerous band,
Now joy in the stones and the dust of their Land.
Their wonderful past they attempt to display
To the Gentiles and strangers they meet in the way.

Alas that the veil remains over their eyes,
Which blinds them to glory come down from the skies!
When Jesus the Christ was at Bethlehem born,
Their nation all faithless turned from Him in scorn.

His claims they rejected, and still they reject,
E'en though His disciples they treat with respect.
But not till the blindness departs from their heart
Will they, can they, cast from them their nation's sore smart.

Till Jesus they know as their Saviour from sin,
They must suffer in measure, nor true joy can win.
God hasten the day when to Israel's nation
Shall come the Lord Jesus who alone is salvation!

8
Chiefly about Masada

O UR stay in the territory of Jordan was followed by a stay of similar duration in the land of Israel, too short for a sight of all places of especial interest, but sufficiently long to yield firm impressions of the land and its people. It would be invidious to set up a comparison between Jordan and Israel. In both places we were well received and housed, fed and guided. Our travel agents had made excellent arrangements with the two sets of nationals so that we were taken expeditiously and comfortably to the places of biblical interest which we were eager to visit. We could not, however, fail to notice the much greater degree of material prosperity that had resulted from the setting up of the Jewish National State in 1948, a phenomenon which has arrested the attention of statesmen and journalists the world over and which undoubtedly justifies one of the latter – Terence Prittie – who has written on Israel very recently, in the use of the phrase, *Miracle in the Desert*. The division of territory which came about in 1948 gave to Israel areas more fertile than those retained by the Arabs of Jordan. Certainly the Negev, stretching from Beersheba to Eilat on the Gulf of Akaba, and about one half of Israel's territory, is largely desert – it has been described as 'lunar landscape' – but the northern half, including the coastal strip, the Vale of Esdraelon, and Galilee is valuable agricultural land, and the 'returning nation' is already reaping the fruits of its financial investments and its arduous labour. Plantations of citrous fruits, figs, apricots, and olives, as we observed times without number, now cover considerable areas of the country, and a long-neglected territory is in process of blossoming as the rose. Jordan suffers from lack of water. Israel is favoured with water, and by skilful irrigation is making the utmost possible use of it.

In addition, the afforestation of the land has been undertaken on a very extensive scale. Approximately a hundred million trees have been planted since 1948, and of these, six million have been planted on the sides of the main road which gives access to Jerusalem from the coast. They have a special commemorative purpose. Each of them keeps green, in the most literal sense, the memory of the six million Jewish victims of the Hitlerite persecution. The road runs through what is now known as the Valley of Martyrs. In addition, though it may sound a very gruesome idea, the various sections of afforested land have been given names taken from German Concentration Camps.

It will not be inappropriate to mention that I am the possessor of a book representing a different mode of commemorating this, the most inhuman form of persecution which has ever befallen the Jewish race. It is a copy of the Book of Esther, elaborately ornate, and measuring twelve inches by nine. Each right-hand page shows the Hebrew text of Esther with highly-coloured pictorial margins, and each left-hand page gives the English translation [Authorized Version] in capital letters of impressive size. It was produced by the Miriam Publishing House of Jerusalem, though the coloured designs are the work of an

English firm located at Banbury. I mention the book because of the pathetic interest attaching to an editorial inscription which it contains, in Hebrew and English: 'In loving memory of my mother, Rivka Reisel Rawicki, who died a martyr's death in the ghetto of Warsaw, a victim of the Haman of our times. May the Lord avenge her soul'. To Jewish hearts the Book of Esther doubtless makes a tremendous appeal in these days. And on his part, the Christian cannot but note that the Lord's purpose of re-populating the Holy Land with a remnant of His ancient people has come about, in part, through the arch-persecutor of modern, and maybe of all, times.

*

We left Jordan in the early hours of a day in mid-May, and passing through the Mandelbaum Gate [inside the City, not a gate in the ancient walls] with a minimum of official formalities, found ourselves in the presence of the descendants of men whose seers and priests and prophets had walked in the light of the Lord when the lands of the West were shrouded in night. In Judah had God been known: His Name had been great in Israel. In Salem had been His tabernacle and His dwelling place in Zion [*Ps.* 76.1–2]. The morning was spent in an all-too-brief tour of the Israeli part of Jerusalem, during which we saw the new Knesset [Parliament] building, near to which on the roadside stood the large seven-branched candelabra presented by the British Parliament [the world's oldest, though some would dispute this] to Israel's Parliament [indisputably the world's youngest], as a gesture of good will. We reflected on the fact that Britain had played a leading part in the promoting of the re-settlement of the Jews in the Land, from the Balfour Declaration of 1917 to the creation of the new Jewish State in 1948.

Interesting, too, it is to recollect that Britain had used its military forces to wrest Palestine from the Turks [backed by German arms] in 1917–18. There seems strong evidence for the belief that the idea of a Palestinian campaign originated with Lloyd George, whose early biblical background – he was a Welsh Baptist – gave him a special interest in the Holy Land. In 1917 he was Prime Minister, and in June of that year he informed General Edmund Allenby, who had been selected to lead the Palestinian Campaign, that 'Jerusalem was wanted as a Christmas present for the British nation'. Viscount Wavell, Allenby's biographer, describes him as a man of 'tremendous personality', who needed every ounce of physical and moral strength which he possessed to lead the forces which drove Turks and Germans from the Land. The ensuing campaigns were brilliantly planned and executed, the fighting forces being drawn from several parts of the Empire. We cannot here enter into details, but Gaza, Beersheba and Megiddo are places which receive chief mention. Suffice it to say that the Bible and George Adam Smith's *Historical Geography of the Holy Land* were always close to Allenby's hand. On one occasion, says Wavell, his Chief of Staff was conducting him through country north of Jerusalem and explaining the disposition of the troops in the area. 'Suddenly The Commander broke out, "Look at that big rock in front of us. That must be just about the place where Jonathan and his armour-bearer climbed up and attacked the Philistine garrison". A graphic description of Jonathan's feat followed [1 *Sam.* 14].' The Chief of Staff then took Allenby to another part of the line, only to receive a detailed description of one of Joshua's battles that had taken place there.

It was the 11th December, 1917, when Allenby made his official entry into Jerusalem. Again I quote Wavell:

Chiefly about Masada

The old historic city, sacred to three of the world's chief religions, had fallen to yet another conqueror. It had often gone down, in blood and ruin; this time its surrender had a touch of comedy. The mayor came out with a white flag to hand over the keys of the great city to the British; he offered them in succession to some cooks of a London regiment who had lost their way, to a sergeant on outpost duty, and to some artillery officers intent on getting their guns into action against the Turkish rearguards. None of these felt themselves quite equal to so historic an occasion. In the end the surrender was accepted by General Shea, the commander of the 60th Division, on behalf of Allenby. Two days later, on December 11, Allenby made his official entry into Jerusalem.

Allenby had entered Jerusalem by the Jaffa Gate on foot. And probably on foot is the best way by far of taking stock of what Jerusalem has to show the visitor. To tour the city by coach, as befell our party, has its pros and cons: all too often, when one wishes to pause, one has to go. A tight timetable has to be maintained. The straggler becomes *non persona grata*, both to his fellow-tourists and to the driver and official guide. It is essential to keep 'with it' in the strictest sense of that much-used term.

Circling the Israeli part of Jerusalem, as aforesaid, we left the candelabra and the Knesset building after due admiration of the latter's architectural qualities. I learned later that the Knesset consists of 120 members, a number based on the size of the Gedola, or Great Assembly, of 2,000 years ago. It is curious that this should also be the same as that of the disciples of the Lord gathered in Jerusalem awaiting 'the Promise of the Father' [*Acts* 1.15]. Shortly we once again found ourselves overlooking the western end of the Kidron Valley. The view was almost as impressive as that of Jerusalem viewed from

Olivet. The conjunction of the Kidron and Hinnom valleys takes place at their lowest points, so that the height of the city walls above the immediately surrounding country towards the south-east is, comparatively, at its greatest. It was at this point that *Psalm* 48 was read to us by our leader [as mentioned in Chapter 1], and Watts' hymn [with its modern chorus] was heartily sung:

> *'Come we that love the Lord,*
> *And let our joys be known;*
> *Join in a song with sweet accord,*
> *And thus surround the throne.*
>
> *We're marching to Zion,*
> *Beautiful, beautiful Zion;*
> *We're marching upward to Zion,*
> *The beautiful city of God.'*

A visit to the traditional Upper Room followed. It was reached by ascending a long outside staircase, and seemed somewhat unrealistic, largely perhaps because it had been built or rebuilt by the Crusaders, and was remote in style from all that one imagines the Upper Room to have been. Where a site cannot be guaranteed as authentic, pre-conceived ideas as to its character determine whether it proves agreeable or not. Between the 'large upper room furnished' and the arched amplitude of the Upper Room of today, contrast rather than comparison proved dominant; but we thought of the poignant occasion when the Lord was 'troubled in spirit', of the paschal feast, of the sop, of the bread and the cup, of the discourse concerning the coming of the Holy Spirit, and for the moment lived in a different world from that of time and sense.

Our next call was at David's tomb in the same block of buildings as the Upper Room. 'David is both dead and buried, and his sepulchre is with us unto this day', says Peter in his Pentecostal sermon. Whether the particular sarcophagus on which we now looked is indeed that of Israel's second king it is impossible to say, but it looks important enough. As the wailing wall, at which for centuries past pious Jews have lamented the departure of Zion's glories, was until June 1967 in the part of the city held by Jordan, David's tomb had taken its place as the scene of 'lamentations and mourning and woe'.

> *'They left thee but a wailing place,*
> *At which to sob thy story,*
> *And mourn with sad averted face*
> *The days of vanished glory'.*

At one time, it seems, no approach to David's tomb was permitted to visitors, but we were allowed to approach to within a yard or two of it. It was covered with a reddish cloth and guarded by a watchful attendant as well as by a strong railing. Jews and Jewesses were given right of complete access, and while we stood and gazed, the sounds of their grief made sad our hearts. We were almost glad to escape into the outer air again.

From Jerusalem we were taken to the sea-coast, calling on the way at Ain Karim, the reputed birthplace of John the Baptist, and therefore the home of Zecharias and Elizabeth, in the 'hill country of Judaea'. A church building of considerable size and beauty now stands there.

*

It had been my strong desire to visit Masada on the western shore of the Dead Sea and in Israeli territory. The difficulty was that a direct journey from Jerusalem to Masada was impossible owing to the block of Jordan territory which protruded between the two places, and it was necessary to make a long detour. Through the kindness of a friend who was at the time staying in Jerusalem and who possessed a reliable car, I had hoped that arrangements could be made, but at the last moment the news reached me that, after all, it was not practicable at that time to make the journey. It is not therefore possible for me to write about Masada as one who has seen the place and taken stock of its strength and significance. Instead I am inserting at this point in my narrative an account of Masada[1] which will, I trust, make good the deficiency. The fact that a Masada Exhibition was held in London in December, 1966, for the benefit of the British people, has recently brought the once famous spot to the public notice. It was a fortress of Herod the Great, the king responsible for the slaughter of the babes of Bethlehem, and almost eighty years after his death was the place where Jewish Zealots made their last stand against the Romans, following upon the fall of Jerusalem in AD 70. Archaeologists did much work there from 1963 to 1965.

Masada, a 'place of gaunt and majestic beauty' is situated close to the Dead Sea at a spot where, in the first century AD, the frontiers of Judaea and Idumaea [the Greek form of the word 'Edom'] were contiguous. It is a kind of Palestinian Gibraltar, an elevated rock eminently suited to be a defensive post, and of such a character that an attacker required the utmost military skill and tenacity if he was to achieve success. The capture of Jerusalem in AD 70 was no easy task even for the most determined and experienced of enemies; for Masada to fall to its foes required an even greater call upon military prowess and endeavour. Hitherto, Flavius Josephus, the Jewish historian of the first century AD, has been the chief, and indeed the only authority, for happenings at Masada, even as it is upon him

---

[1] Written for the *Bible League Quarterly* [Spring, 1967].

also that we depend for our detailed knowledge of the siege and fall of Jerusalem. But now the spade of the archaeologist is able to correct Josephus in certain ways, a surprising thing after well-nigh two thousand years of change and decay.

The story begins with the fortification of Masada by Herod the Great. Actually, according to Josephus, 'Jonathan the High Priest' – scholars are not absolutely certain which of two Jonathans is meant – made the first attempt to fortify Masada, but it was Herod who, about thirty years before the Lord's birth, commenced building work there on a vast scale. It was obviously in his mind to construct a fortress-residence to which he might retreat or retire whenever the mood seized him, or whenever the political horizon became black with clouds. Josephus hints at two kinds of danger; first, that arising from the Jews themselves who, one may judge, must have felt Herod's rule to be harshly oppressive; second, it appears that the famous Cleopatra, Queen of Egypt, was anxious to obtain possession of Judaea, and to this end urged her lover, Mark Anthony, the friend of Julius Caesar, to destroy Herod; but apparently the opportunity did not present itself. Herod, however, scented ever-present danger, and Masada was his rock of refuge. God, said the Psalmist, is 'the rock of my refuge' [*Ps.* 94.22]. Herod had no such defence. Maybe he hoped that, if things came to the worst, he could escape from Masada into his native Idumaea, despite the curse which Isaiah had pronounced upon that land [*Isa.* 34.5]. Perhaps we do not give too much play to imagination if we suppose that Herod, ensconced in his all but impregnable palace-residence, gave his own interpretation to further words of *Isaiah* [33.16]: 'He shall dwell on high [literally so]; His place of defence shall be the munitions of rocks; bread shall be given him [he built storechambers where he stored up abundant supplies of food]; his waters shall be sure' [with enormous labour, rock-hewn cisterns were constructed, to contain the occasional deluge which visited this parched wilderness country].

Masada was not merely one of a series of Herodian fortresses which included Herodion [a little to the south of Bethlehem] and Machaerus [where John the Baptist was later imprisoned and beheaded] which occupied a site in Peraea, on the opposite side of the Dead Sea from Masada. From the first, Herod intended it to be a royal residence, sumptuously equipped, where his subjects might contemplate him as 'a king in his beauty', dwelling in 'the land that is very far off' [*Isa.* 33.17]. With immense labour he reared a complex of buildings on the top of the rock. They included a casemate wall of dressed stone which made the complete circuit of the summit and was not much less than a mile in length. It was covered with white plaster, which causes Josephus erroneously to state that it was of white stone. Thirty-eight towers were built on the wall and within them and the wall itself were over a hundred rooms, some of them of considerable size. In the west-centre of the lozenge-shaped summit a palace was erected. It contained a throne room and was clearly intended to serve as the official residence of the king from which the business of the Kingdom could be conveniently [or, as far as subjects were concerned, inconveniently] transacted. Three smaller palaces stood nearby, complete with swimming pool.

At the northern end of the rock was built, with incredible labour, a three-tiered palace-villa, Herod's private residence, upon which he bestowed his utmost care and thought. Josephus describes it, but the recent excavations of Dr Yigael Yadin, Professor of Archaeology in the Hebrew University of Jerusalem, have added very considerably to our knowledge. The residence was built literally on the edge of an abyss, and to render the building possible, large supporting walls up to eighty feet high were constructed. This enabled the king to build at three levels, the lowest being a hundred feet below the summit, and the middle tier sixty feet. Magnificent frescoes supplied ornamentation, and no effort was spared to render the building 'exceeding magnifical'. A bath house contained a *frigidarium* [cold room], a *tepidarium* [tepid room], a *caldarium* [hot room], and an *apoditerium* [disrobing room]. Heat was supplied by the use of a hypocaust after the approved Roman fashion. Storerooms – about fourteen in number – stood side by side in rectangular pattern. Each such room contained one commodity – oil, wine, flour, and so on. Certainly Herod's garrison could have sustained a long siege if it had been be-leagured in Masada. Some of the sherds of broken wine jars found by the archaeologists bore the name of the Roman consul for the year 19 BC [C. Sentius Saturninus] and supplied the added words, 'To King Herod of Judaea'. This particular vintage had been sent to the king from Italy. This is the first time that archaeology has yielded an inscription with the name of Herod.

We cannot doubt that Herod had chosen the precipitous northern face of the rock from purely personal motives. Heat with wind came from the south, even as Christ reminded certain hypocrites [*Luke* 12.55]. To the north of Masada's summit was shade and shelter, and Herod was consulting his own comfort by requiring his engineers to construct his private residence in an almost impossible, and certainly for them a highly dangerous spot. But the views were wonderful.

One of the most interesting of the finds on Masada was that of a synagogue, the original Herodian building having been modified by the Zealots who took possession and defied the Romans. Without doubt this is the earliest synagogue discovered in Israel. It was oriented towards Jerusalem as required by 'the tradition of the elders'. Embedded in its floor was found an ostracon [potsherd] inscribed 'Priestly tithe', together with many vessels, including a wash-basin. But the most interesting aspect of this discovery was that of a piece of rolled scroll. It was found in what the Jews termed a 'geniza', a pit specially dug to receive copies of sacred writings which were no longer usable, either through age or tattered condition or because use had revealed copyists' mistakes. The Jews could not bring themselves to destroy such scrolls any more than Bible-loving Christians today can find it in their hearts to do away with Bibles which have become defaced and soiled.

The scrolls discovered at Masada contained a part of the Prophecy of Ezekiel, and included [mirabile dictu] chapter 37 with its vision of the dry bones. It was a find which seemed strangely remindful of the miracle which constitutes Israel's sad but wonderful story. Spiritually, Israel has been for long centuries a dry-bone nation which recently, by a significant national re-awakening linked with the movement known as Zionism, has returned to its own land after a 'captivity' lasting wellnigh two millenniums. Alas that it still remains blind [though only in part: *Rom.* 11.25] to the true cause of the divine wrath which rendered its land and its people desolate! Yet if Israel has not yet risen spiritually from its ancient grave, the day has dawned when 'the stone shall cry out of the wall, and the beam out of the timber shall answer it'.

A further exciting discovery was made in one of the rooms of the casemate wall. Under much debris a collection of miscellaneous articles was found, including vessels, mats, baskets and leatherware, together with seventeen silver shekels in excellent condition, all dated from the period immediately before the fall of Jerusalem and inscribed 'Jerusalem the holy'. Near by was a

piece of creased and blackened parchment which contained
Psalms 81 to 85. By the use of infra-red rays – all the great
libraries employ this method for getting at the obscure contents of old parchments – they could be deciphered with comparative ease, and, says Dr Yadin, 'like the other biblical scrolls
which we found later, this section from the *Book of Psalms* is
almost exactly identical [except for a few very minor changes
here and there] to the text of the biblical books which we use
today. Even the division into chapters and psalms is identical
with the traditional division'.

In the same locality the diggers discovered two fragments of
the *Book of Leviticus*, and elsewhere a copy of *Psalm* 150:
'Praise ye the Lord ... Praise Him with the sound of the trumpet'. 'The writing was so faded', runs the record, 'and the colour
of the parchment so light that it almost escaped our notice, and
indeed when it was being cleaned one of the volunteers thought
what she was holding in her hand was a piece of newspaper'.
Actually it was a scrap of white leather.

Another discovery was that of a part of a scroll which contained the *Apocryphal Book of Ecclesiasticus*, dated in the first
half of the first century BC. Still another, described by Dr Yadin
for certain reasons as 'an archaeological miracle', was a copy of
chapters 8 to 12 of *Leviticus*. This scroll, he adds, 'was absolutely identical with the traditional text of *Leviticus*. Moreover,
there was the same division into sections, the traditional division into "open" and "closed" ones, that is, sections which
begin after an empty line-space at the end of the previous one,
and those which begin after a small space in the same line'. The
discovery of this fragment seemed to be simplicity itself. It
happened on the first day of the second season of excavation.
A young lad from a kibbutz [communal settlement] in Galilee,
pottering about among surface debris, discovered the *Leviticus*

fragments scattered around, apparently on or very near the surface, and to the amazement of workers they could be immediately identified and read. It was surmised that they had been blown to the spot of their discovery by the wind or thrown there by an uninterested Roman soldier after the capture of the fortress.

*

The story of the capture of the palace-fortress is gruesome in the extreme. It took place shortly after the siege and fall of Jerusalem and its temple as prophesied by the Lord [*Luke* 19.41–44; 21.6]. Four years before the Holy City was captured by Titus in the year 70, a group of Jewish Zealots had captured Masada from the Roman garrison which then held it. After the fall of their capital they were joined by a few desperate men who had somehow evaded the Roman patrols and had survived the hazardous thirty-mile journey southwards to the Judaea – Idumaea border. It did not consist with Rome's pride of arms to permit this last pocket of resistance to continue, and in AD 72 the Roman Governor, Flavius Silva, laid siege to 'the rock'. The Tenth Legion was served by thousands of Jewish prisoners who had no option but to labour without respite for the overthrow of their brethren. Supply lines had to be constructed and maintained, no less than eight camps had to be built, and – most hated task of all perhaps – Masada had to be completely surrounded by a wall over two miles long to prevent the escape of the beleaguered. But the Roman general was not content merely to watch and wait until at long last the Zealots were starved into surrender. He contrived a means to break into the fortress. A huge ramp was constructed up the western side of the rock. It can still be seen, little changed from the time of its construction. It enabled the Romans to use battering rams and other military machines against the Jewish wall of defence.

It is to Josephus that we again have to turn for a detailed account of the awful horrors that ensued. His narrative seems highly dependable and includes an account of the last desperate measures taken by the besieged to rob the Romans of some of the joys of victory. The Jewish commander was Eleazar ben Yair. When the Romans had completed their ramp and reached the walls of the fortress, it was soon realized by the defenders that, within days or even hours, the final break-through by the attackers would take place. Eleazar thereupon decided that it was preferable for the Jews to die by their own hand rather than die at Roman hands or live to grace a Roman triumph. Josephus supplies us with the speech by which he persuaded his fellow-soldiers and their wives to accept such a fate and to die bravely. Presumably he learned its content from two Jewish women who, together with five children, escaped by hiding. There were 960 people in Masada at the time of its fall. The final act of desperation Josephus describes thus:

> *They then chose ten men by lot out of them to slay all the rest: everyone of whom laid himself down by his wife and children on the ground, and threw his arms about them, and they offered their necks to the stroke of those who by lot executed that melancholy office. And when these ten men had, without fear, slain them all, they made the same rule for casting lots for themselves, that he whose lot it was to first kill the other nine, after all, should kill himself.*

It seems likely that the archaeologists have discovered the very ostraca which were used in the casting of the lots. Eleven have come to light, different from all other such finds in Masada. One of them is inscribed 'Ben Ya'ir' and it is highly probable that this is the lot of Eleazar himself, the commander who survived to the bitter end. The mortal remains of the dead have

been found, in part, and include one of the most pitiable finds of all, the plaited hair still attached to the skull of a young woman whose skeleton was found near that of a warrior and child. Her leather sandals were not far away.

Already, before the capture of Masada, to commemorate the triumph over Jewry, Rome had issued a special coin inscribed 'Judaea capta'. It depicted a captive Jewish woman in the garments and posture of extreme grief. Behind her [doubtless to assist in identification] is a palm tree, and behind the palm tree a Roman soldier in an attitude of triumph.

Six-and-a-half centuries before Jerusalem and Masada fell to the Romans, Jerusalem had fallen to the Babylonians, and a similar state of affairs had prevailed. I close this chapter by quoting a small part of the Lament uttered by Jeremiah on that occasion:

Is it nothing to you, all ye that pass by? Behold and see if there be any sorrow like unto my sorrow, which is done unto me, wherewith the Lord hath afflicted me in the day of His fierce anger.

GALILEE

Four chosen brethren here,
    (But humble fishers then)
Soon as Thy word they hear,
    Fishers become of men.

One from his ship by night
    Walked fearless on the wave;
Him did wild winds affright,
    He called on Thee to save.

His was the walk of faith;
    From unbelief his fear;
Sinking those waves beneath,
    He prayed, and found Thee near.

As once from opening clouds
    Manna Thy people fed;
So here to listening crowds
    Thou gavest daily bread:

Where flowers yon waters meet,
    Hid truths Thou didst unfold,
More precious and more sweet
    Than honey or than gold.

Here Peter's broken net
    The preacher's weakness shows;
Thy power before him set,
    He sought to hide sin's woes.

'Depart from me, O Lord;
    A sinful man am I.'
Scared at Thy powerful word,
    Such still the heart's deep cry.

Soon comfort came, then strength;
    Now Thou forbid'st his fear;
Risen from the grave at length,
    Again they find Thee here.

No more their net shall break
    For fifty thrice and three;
When bold Thy word they speak,
    Nations shall gathered be.

Aid Thou Thy servants, Lord,
    Wisely their net to cast;
All seasons suit Thy word,
    Till life's long night is past.

H. B. WHITAKER CHURTON

In the fourth chapter of the Gospel of John we are told concerning the Lord that 'He left Judaea and departed again into Galilee; and He must needs go through Samaria' [4.3–4]. For a very different reason, we who now wished to travel from Jerusalem to the shores of the Lake must needs go through Jaffa and Tel Aviv. The strangely drawn frontier of 1948 – as it existed at the time of our visit – left us with no alternative, except to skirt these cities without visiting them.

En route we passed close to the site of ancient Kirjath-jearim [city of forests] where the ark rested for twenty years in 'the house of Abinadab in the hill' [1 *Sam.* 6.21], having been retained for a time in what we now call 'the Gaza strip', then the country of the Philistines, who had captured it in battle. When it was returned to Israel on a new cart drawn by two milch kine, 'lowing as they went', it arrived at Beth-shemesh, but a judgment inflicted on the men of that place for their irreverence caused them to invite the men of Kirjath-jearim to take the ark to their village. This they did. To our eyes the site pointed out to us looked pleasant in the extreme, but we had no opportunity to give it more than a passing glance.

Jaffa [Joppa], now virtually a suburb of Tel Aviv [Hill of Spring] – a case of an extremely old city being linked to an extremely new one – provided a particularly happy visit, if only for the fact that we had a most interesting reminder of an event narrated in the *Acts of the Apostles*. Jaffa itself seemed to hold no special attraction. Such streets as we saw were somewhat shabby in appearance; maybe we missed the more attractive thoroughfares, if such there were. But as compensation we arrived at the house of Simon the tanner by the sea-side, and immediately felt ourselves 'at home' in the sense that we saw almost precisely what we had expected to see – a squat flat-roofed house, an outer staircase leading to the house-top, and in front the blue waters of the far-reaching 'Great Sea'. It would be naive to believe this to be the very house of *Acts*, chapter ten, but at least it stood at the right spot and was doubtless much after the pattern of the tanner's dwelling.

It was not at all difficult to imagine a hungry apostle resting on the house-top as he awaited his mid-day meal. Equally easy was it to visualize the arrival of the 'two household servants and a soldier' sent by Cornelius, and to hear [by supposition] their knocking at the gate. Our own knocking had brought out a lady to inquire our purpose. She readily gave us permission to ascend the staircase and look around from that point of vantage. It was a rewarding view, and we tended to linger unduly, until reminded that we were still a long way from Galilee and our final destination.

The coastal plain along which we now travelled northwards was a true highway of nations. Its fertility, marked today by its numerous orange groves, was not, however, the chief reason for its attractiveness to the great States of the ancient world.

Rather did it provide the Egyptians with means of access to the upper Euphrates Valley and Mesopotamia. To the Assyrians and Babylonians it was the route to be followed if Egypt was to be entered. Along this plain, in old times known as Sharon, the chariots and horsemen of hostile powers had passed, south to north and north to south, times without number. And when the Eastern powers had had their day, Western powers had entered the land. In turn, Greek and Roman had held sway and, when the whirligig of time had for them run its course, Seljuk Turk and Crusader had, centuries later, added to the historic pattern long before modern times were reached. And what of today?

Peter had returned with the inquirers who arrived at Simon the tanner's house and had travelled with them to Caesarea, twenty-five miles away. We followed their steps, and duly arrived at the place where Rome had fixed her Palestinian headquarters. No building is now to be identified as the house of Cornelius. It was in this spot six years ago that a tablet was found which included the first archaeological occurrence of the name of Pontius Pilate, procurator of Judaea. In Caesarea, too, lived Philip the evangelist and his daughters [*Acts* 21.8–9]. Paul was a prisoner here for two years, awaiting trial and finally appealing to Caesar. Here too it was that he spoke before Felix, Festus, and King Agrippa. Caesarea had a prominent part to play in the Christian story. Certain of the ruins date from the time of the Crusaders who built a fortress here. Walls of great strength, together with a moat, filled from the sea, are still to be seen. They cover a considerable area. Our guide gave us to understand that Richard Coeur de Lion was responsible for their construction, but it was not easy to assimilate this claim. Richard was in the Holy Land from June, 1191 to October, 1192, but during that period he was engaged in almost incessant warfare and it seems most unlikely that he could have devoted attention to the construction of the walls on which we stood.

In an earlier crusade in 1101, Caesarea is said to have been the place where a hexagonal vase of green crystal was found, and legend has it that this had been used at the Last Supper. As 'the holy grail' [cup] it played an important part in mediaeval story. Thus does Caesarea hold to view the strength of mediaeval superstitions.

Certain of the remains of old Caesarea are under water. It was Herod the Great who turned the shore at this point into a seaport. In fact he was the founder of Caesarea, named thus by him in honour of the Emperor Augustus [about 13 BC]. It became the most important site in Palestine. In it Herod built an amphitheatre to seat 20,000 spectators. It remains magnificent in ruins. Aqueducts supplied the town with water. Their picturesque grandeur still adorns the coast. The site of Caesarea remains in fact 'an archaeologist's dream'.

*

Our route next led us northwards past and over the range of Carmel into the Plain of Esdraelon. We skirted the hills on which Nazareth stands, passed Mount Tabor on our left, climbed again and shortly had our first sight of the Sea of Galilee. Our destination was Ginosar, a spot on the western side of the Sea, mid-way between Tiberias and Capernaum.

Galilee is a delightful part of the Holy Land. Its rolling hills have their own charms, especially in the springtime before the sun with burning heat has begun its summer's race. The grass is green, flowers abound, and it is indeed a 'delightsome' land [*Mal.* 3.12]. The delights of the Sea add much to its beauty. In Scripture it is, of course, given a variety of names – Chinnereth in the Old Testament [the name still appears on signposts in the neighbourhood], Gennesaret, Galilee, and the Sea of Tiberias in the New. It is doubtless correct to claim that its Old Testament name, basically meaning a harp, derives from the shape of the Sea which roughly corresponds to the shape of the harp of the ancient world. It is certainly not a sea in the oceanic sense of that word, for it is a mere thirteen miles in length, and seven in breadth at the most. It is difficult to compare it for size with British inland waters for those which come most readily to mind possess length rather than breadth. Bala, the largest sheet of natural water in Wales [a country comparable for size with Palestine] is very small in comparison with Galilee, a mere four miles by two-thirds of a mile. Windermere, 'the noblest stretch of water in England', is a little over ten miles in length but only a mile in breadth. In Scotland Loch Ness is twice as long as Galilee, but again only a mile in average width. Loch Lomond at its widest reaches to five miles but it contains numerous islands and it is impossible to draw a comparison. The nearest counterpart in the British Isles is Lough Neagh in Northern Ireland, which measures some fourteen miles by ten.

The fact is that the Sea of Galilee is comparatively small. Today, when few live on its shores, it presents a great contrast with its ancient state, when its coasts were as full of men as its waters with fish. The fish remain, but, surprisingly, men are few. In Bible days, when it was 'Galilee of the Gentiles', the population appears to have been well distributed around the Lake on both its eastern and western shores. Today Israel has concentrated attention on her Mediterranean seaboard, and the shores of the Lake still await the sowing with the seed of men and with the seed of beast foretold by the weeping prophet [*Jer.* 31.27]. One present difficulty is that, though the Lake – I use the terms Lake and Sea here indiscriminately – is wholly

Israel's, she does not control the eastern shore which, but for an extremely narrow strip, belongs to the State of Syria; the strip widens somewhat from En Gev southwards.

We found ourselves accommodated in the hotel belonging to a kibbutz [Ginosar] and which has been built to accommodate tourists. It is situated at the point where the Sea attains its maximum width. The hotel was as comfortable as could be desired and the food excellent. As in Jordan, each apartment or chalet possessed its own shower and toilet. Situated on the shore of the Sea, and with water easy of access, such members of our party as were devoted to bathing were in their element. The eucalyptus trees and banana plantations in the immediate locality gave a semi-tropical aspect to this area. At Jerusalem we sampled the benefits of city life; here we enjoyed the lush and tranquil beauty of the hills and the shining levels of the Lake. Sunrise and sunset were hours of more than ordinary loveliness, especially the former when a path of glory stretched across the waters, reminding one of Mrs Julia Ward Howe's words, 'He is coming like the glory of the morning on the wave'. Alas that as these pages are being written the peace of the land is being rudely disturbed by conflict, and the words are the rather being fulfilled, 'He is trampling out the vintage where the grapes of wrath are stored'. Yet comfort springs from the remembrance of the divine promise [*Jer.* 30.7]: 'It is even the time of Jacob's trouble: but he shall be saved out of it'. And with this verse we link another: 'Even so come, Lord Jesus' [*Rev.* 22.20].

The hills that look down upon the Lake are in themselves abodes of peace. Nature was at its loveliest at the time of our arrival, with combinations of yellows and reds, buttercups and poppies. Yet there is much to remind of the primeval curse pronounced upon the ground for man's sake. Thistles flourish, some of them as high as men, with thorns of the most awesome prickliness. Some of the smaller plants also have most formidable spikes, and the hand that dares to touch them has to beware of the beauty thus protected. Yet in the deserts of the south, where camels feed, they make nothing of thorn and prickle. I did not myself see them grazing [if this is the appropriate term to use], but General Allenby, writing to his wife in 1917, speaks thus:

> *I was astounded today to see the camels browsing on prickly-pear cactus. I had always thought that the prickly pear was proof against any animal that had a palate and a tongue. But I see the camels eating it greedily, and paying no more heed to the awful spines than if they were bloom on a peach.*

*

One morning I took a stroll along the lakeside and then climbed up the lower slopes of one of the Horns of Hattin. The Horns are two peaks of similar height and joined by a saddle; they are sufficiently close together to count as one mountain. Here in July, 1187, Guy de Lusignan, crusading King of Jerusalem, had met with defeat at the hands of Saladin, a defeat so calamitous that George Adam Smith comments: 'A militant and truculent Christianity, as false as the relics of the "true cross" round which it was rallied, met its judicial end, within view of the scenes where Christ proclaimed the Gospel of Peace and went about doing good.' It is difficult to grasp the exact import of 'judicial end', for four years later Richard of England and Philip Augustus of France arrived in the Holy Land to begin the third crusade, though it is certainly true that they failed to recover the lands previously held by the Crusaders.

Dr Edward Robinson of New York, visiting the Holy Land

in 1838, was in Galilee in the month of June, but confesses that he found little in the landscape to attract the eye. His words run thus: 'The hills are rounded and tame, with little of the picturesque in their form; they are decked by no shrubs nor forests; and even the verdure of the grass and herbage, which earlier in the season might give them a pleasing aspect, was already gone; they were now only naked and dreary. Whoever looks here for the magnificence of the Swiss Lakes or the softer beauty of those of England and the United States, will be disappointed'.

My own impression is different from this. Granted that our visit was in the month of May, and not when the month of June had begun 'to burn as an oven'; but even so, there was a quiet beauty in the contour of the hills and in the combination of sea and land which could not vary with the season of the year. The knowledge that the feet of the Lord during thirty and more years trod the hillsides, the valleys, the shores of this particular Sea, and even the Sea itself, also gave it a charm and a power over the mind which no other scene in the wide world could convey. M'Cheyne speaks of seeing Galilee 'sleeping as calmly and softly as if it had been the sea of glass which John saw in heaven'. He continues: 'We felt an indescribable interest even in lifting a shell from the shore of a sea where Jesus had so often walked'.

But to return to the Horns of Hattin! After selecting with care the usual stone of memorial, together with specimens of thistles and other plants, I descended the mountain and met with difficulty in finding my way to the coastal road again. Between mountain and road were widespread vineyards with numerous irrigation ditches, and my failure to note with sufficient care the exact line of my approach caused me to get 'entangled in the land' as I returned. I mention the matter because of its sequel. I finally came across a youth of about seventeen years who was engaged in attending to the irrigation pipes. He not only gave me directions for my disentanglement but said that he would accompany me, as he was himself about to return to a kibbutz in the neighbourhood. He understood English sufficiently well to make sense of my words, and informed me that he knew well both Arabic, his native language [he was Moslem], and Hebrew. Before we parted he had given me evidence that his measure of learning was not to be despised. I had handed to him a Scripture Gift Mission booklet entitled 'The Good Shepherd', and he commenced to read it aloud. 'Shepherd' proved slightly difficult, but, this surmounted, he proceeded to read the Psalm which followed:

> *Know ye that the Lord He is God: it is He that hath made us, and not we ourselves; we are His people and the sheep of His pasture.*

Naturally 'ye' and 'hath' presented a little further difficulty, but it was clear to me that he understood not only the outward sound of the words, but also their import. I was duly impressed. How many English youths, comparable to him in age, would be able to converse in three languages and, as was doubtless true in his case, to read them intelligently from a printed text? Before we parted company a small group of his fellows who approached us had shown interest in the booklet and had settled down to the perusal of a second copy.

*

Our visit to the district of Capernaum was a pleasant episode. It commenced with the ascent of the Mount of Beatitudes, now surmounted by a hospice, and the reading of the first part of the Sermon on the Mount. It was easy to imagine the scene as described with much economy of words by Matthew: 'There followed Him great multitudes of people from Galilee, and from Decapolis, and from Jerusalem, and from Judaea, and from beyond Jordan' . . . 'and when He was set, His disciples came unto Him'. The scene is different today. The throngs have given place to the few. But the same hills, the same sea, and the same blue vault above them are to be seen, and, the world over, the needs of disciples are still being met by the same Lord, even though He is, for a 'little while' – or in the prophet's phrase, for 'a small moment' – hid from the eyes of men.

Not far from the Mount of the Sermon was Tabgha where stands the Church of the Multiplication, said to date from the fourth century, built upon or close to the spot where the Feeding of the Five Thousand took place. It was remarkable for its size and its simplicity. We inspected ancient Byzantine mosaics showing what appeared to be a basket containing loaves with a fish on either side. In the near neighbourhood were the ruins of the Capernaum synagogue, a few of the columns and walls of which still stand. It is hardly to be supposed that the ruins are those of the synagogue in which Christ Himself ministered the Word and performed miracles, but they may stand upon the site of that synagogue, and they certainly call to mind the fact that it was a Roman centurion who met the expense of the building mentioned in the Gospels. The remnants of the building bear an essentially Graeco-Roman character. In muted eloquence they 'cry out' the Gospel of the crucified, risen and ascended Lord, and remind the Christian, and indeed the unbeliever also, that Capernaum was, by virtue of the presence and ministry of the Lord, 'exalted to heaven'. It is far different today and is only worthy to rank with the city of Tyre as a spot, once extremely populous, where now a few fishers spread their nets. There is a small jetty, from which we sailed to Tiberias, pleased for the moment to be afloat on a 'sea of glass', but mindful of the sudden squalls which notoriously whip the ripples into fury and make navigation perilous for open boats. As we cruised peacefully on, our leader read the story of the storm on the lake, and thus stirred our recollections of the occasion when the naked word of One who was Master of wind and water caused the waves to crouch like whipped dogs at His feet. But on this occasion it was needless for us to hear 'Peace, be still', except in the heart, for our brief voyage was, like a certain poet's garden, 'the veriest school of peace'. We tried to sing a hymn each verse of which ended [or at least the chorus ended] with 'Peace, be still; peace, be still'; but most of us knew neither words nor tune, so that, regrettably, hosannas died upon our lips. Yet we were thankful for the opportunity to sail upon 'the Syrian sea', and to call to mind at such close quarters the chain of miracles which had stirred its depths, brought tranquillity to its surface, and rendered its shores for ever a scene of wonder to the Christian. The joy was tempered only by the reflection that from the hills which border its eastern shores, political hatreds still flare up periodically into military episodes.

*

During one of our journeys we visited a kibbutz [plural: kibbutzim] and made a brief tour of inspection. The oldest of such settlements is that at Dagania at the southern end of the Sea of Galilee, and it is by their means that in recent years the development of the land in respect of agriculture, fisheries, irrigation and forestry has made astonishing progress. Property in the kibbutzim is communally owned, and work is organized on a collective basis. 'The members', states Gerald de Gaury in *The New State of Israel* [1952], give their labour to the common stock and receive from the settlement the satisfaction of their needs in accordance with the financial means of the settlement. Domestic and social services are provided communally; there

is a central dining-room and kitchen, communal kindergarten
and children's quarters, communal social and cultural halls,
library and central supply stores. Married living quarters give
the members some privacy. There are fixed evening hours in
which parents play with their children. Life in a kibbutz is
found in practice to be well suited only to those brought up to
it, and the tendency in consequence is to take only the young,
and to wean future members to the life as children. The population in a kibbutz ranges from sixty in the smallest to two
thousand in the largest'.

There are various types of settlements. They result from the
efforts made by the central government of Israel to re-settle the
land with the former resident Jewish population augmented
by immigrants gathered from the four corners of the earth.
Co-operative settlements tend to rival kibbutzim in popularity,
the first of its kind being set up in 1921 at Nahalal. Most of them
go by the name of Moshav [plural: Moshavim]. In these each
member cultivates his own small holding and pledges himself
not to engage outside labour. He also promises not to engage in
business activity outside the settlement. His chief contribution
is labour. Land, credits, repayments, marketing, distribution of
profits – all these are arranged by the 'co-operative'.

I endeavoured to engage in conversation two or three members of the kibbutz which we visited and to find out what
arrangements applied in matters of religion, but those I approached seemed somewhat mystified. One of them, who
spoke a little English, excused himself by saying that, if it was
a question of religion, his knowledge of the English language
was too slight to enable him to converse with me. I introduced
the word 'synagogue' in the hope of discovering whether this
type of building was known in the kibbutzim or moshavim,
but met with no response. Nor when I enquired about belief in

God in the most general terms did I meet with anything but the rejoinder, so far as I could understand it, that God was not needed by the Israeli.

But certainly the material progress in the settlements was impressive. The numerous buildings were soundly constructed and maintained, there was a neatness and cleanliness on all hands, and it was clear that agriculture was in a flourishing state. The Jew had done more than re-occupy the land; with much skill and vigour he was subduing it to his material needs, tickling it with his hoe till it laughed with a harvest.

*

It is often remarked that there are three chief religious communities in Palestine today – Jewish, Moslem and Christian. In a total population of two and a quarter million, the vast majority, of course, are officially Jewish in religion. But there are also some 200,000 Moslems, approximately 60,000 Christians [using that term in its broadest sense] and about 30,000 Druses, whose religion consists of a strange mixture of Jewish, Christian and Moslem elements. The Druses believe that on ten occasions God has been manifest on earth in human form. Each year they make, representatively, a pilgrimage to the supposed tomb of Jethro, Moses' father-in-law, somewhere near the Horns of Hattin. But how they establish connection with Jethro it is difficult to say. Their origin is much disputed. Some suppose them to be Arabs from the Yemen; others, Kurds, and others describe them as of Chinese stock.

The Jews proper fall into two distinct groups. There are those, a minority, who are strictly orthodox, and seek to practise the Mosaic law. They dress in sombre fashion, keep Sabbath rigorously, study the Old Testament and the Mishna and

Talmud with diligence, and practise self-discipline. They attempt this increasingly as they see the non-religious elements in the State turn to agnosticism and atheism. The synagogue to them becomes not only a place of worship and religious exercise; it is the cultural, social and ethical centre of their lives. They have difficulty in practising all aspects of the Mosaic law. How for instance can they leave their farming land fallow every seventh year under the law of Shemittah, and yet compete with their non-religious neighbours? They seek a solution in a variety of ways. Some of them cut off a corner of their fields and leave it fallow for the required term, on the same principle as that of the offering of the wave-sheaf, which sanctifies the entire harvest. Others arrange a legal transfer [with private reservations on both sides] to a non-Jew for the Sabbatic Year. Cultivation continues uninterruptedly, but the religious Jew is no longer responsible to God for what happens. He receives his land back again at the year-end. There are also other ways by which a fictitious conscience-salving arrangement can be made. And thus does orthodoxy find rest!

The non-religious Jew, resting in his agnosticism or atheism, usually respects or even venerates the Old Testament, not least when he pays it scant attention. He realizes that in a manner inexplicable to him the history of his nation is bound up in its pages, and its future is also enigmatically linked with its prophecies. In the most vague of ways he may even entertain his own version of the Messianic hope, interpreting it solely in terms of earthly good. But of the Christian Gospel of Hope he knows nothing, and for it he cares nothing. Life for him is essentially mundane. Eternal values are hollow. The rule of thumb represented by 'one to his farm and another to his merchandise' has more sway with him than ethical principles or a Gospel bound up with the Person and work of a crucified, risen and ascended Messiah. His utopia is to be found, so he believes, in this present world. Shekel, not shekinah, represents his standard of values. Blindness has happened to him, and none can cure it but the Deliverer coming out of Zion.

THE SEA OF GALILEE

How pleasant to me thy deep blue wave,
    O sea of Galilee!
For the glorious One who came to save
    Hath often stood by thee.

Fair are the lakes in the land I love,
    Where pine and heather grow;
But thou hast loveliness far above
    What Nature can bestow.

It is not that the wild gazelle
    Comes down to drink thy tide,
But He that was pierced to save from hell
    Oft wandered by thy side.

It is not that the fig-tree grows,
    And palms, in thy soft air,
But that Sharon's fair and bleeding Rose
    Once spread its fragrance there.

Graceful around thee the mountains meet,
    Thou calm reposing sea;
But ah! far more, the beautiful feet
    Of Jesus walked o'er thee.

These days are past – Bethsaida where?
    Chorazin, where art thou?
His tent the wild Arab pitches there,
    The wild reeds shade thy brow.

Tell me, ye mouldering fragments, tell
    Was the Saviour's city here?
Lifted to heaven, has it sunk to hell,
    With none to shed a tear?

Ah! would my flock from thee might learn
    How days of grace will flee!
How all an offered Christ who spurn,
    Shall mourn at last, like thee!

And was it beside this very sea
    The risen Saviour said
Three times to Simon, 'Lovest thou Me?
    My lambs and sheep, then, feed'.

O Saviour, gone to God's right hand!
    Yet the same Saviour still,
Graved on Thy heart is this lovely strand
    And every fragrant hill.

Oh! give me, Lord, by this sacred wave,
Threefold Thy love divine,
That I may feed, till I find my grave,
Thy flock — both Thine and mine.

ROBERT MURRAY M'CHEYNE

Sea of Galilee
July 16, 1839

10

We explore Galilee

GALILEE proper is separated from the central highlands of Israel by the extensive plain known in its eastern stretches as the Valley of Jezreel and elsewhere as the Plain of Esdraelon, though the latter name is but the Greek equivalent of the former. The River Kishon – 'that ancient river, the river Kishon' [*Judges* 5.21] – fed by tributaries from the hills both of Galilee and Samaria, waters the plain and enters the Mediterranean Sea in the neighbourhood of Acre. The entire area is replete with the stuff of history, both biblical and secular. It was of vital importance in the line of communication between the Nile and the Euphrates in ancient times. Geographically it linked the Egyptian with the Assyrian, Babylonian and Persian Empires. It was a battleground of nations.

'What a plain it is!', wrote George Adam Smith, 'Upon which not only the greatest empires, races and faiths, east and west, have contended with each other, but each has come to judgment – on which from the first, with all its splendour of human battle, men have felt that *there was fighting from heaven, the stars in their courses were fighting* – on which panic has descended so mysteriously upon the best equipped and most successful armies, but the humble have been exalted to victory in the hour of their weakness – on which false faiths, equally with false defenders of the true faith, have been exposed and scattered – on which since the time of Saul, wilfulness and superstition, though aided by every human excellence, have come to nought, and since Josiah's time the purest piety has not atoned for rash and mistaken zeal. The Crusaders repeat the splendid folly of the kings of Israel; and, alike under the old and the new covenant, a degenerate church suffers here her judgment at the hands of the infidel.

' "They go forth unto the kings of the earth and of the whole world to gather them to the battle of the great day of God Almighty . . . and He gathered them together unto a place called in the Hebrew tongue, Har Megeddon" '.

Armageddon [for such is the usual spelling], the hill of Megiddo, is virtually a synonym for this Plain of Esdraelon, for overlooking it stands one of the most historic fortresses on the face of the earth – Megiddo [now called Lejjun], located on the range of hills terminating in Carmel. Megiddo was a stronghold in the days of the Canaanites and illustrative of the 'formidable civilization which the Israelites under Joshua had to encounter when they invaded the land'. Its water supply was obtained in a fashion similar to that already described in the case of Gibeon, that is to say, by means of a shaft descended by a circular stair round its side. From its base a long tunnel led to a spring of water. A remarkable circular Canaanitish altar of unhewn stones, mounted by a stair of unhewn stones, has been excavated in recent years. At Megiddo Solomon built a new fortress and provided accommodation in it for chariot horses [1 *Kings* 9.15]. Between three and four centuries later Josiah was slain there as he contested the passage of

Egyptian forces under Pharaoh-Necho who was going to the help of the Assyrians [2 *Kings* 23.29].

At Megiddo we found that a museum had been opened for the display of objects of antiquarian interest. In it was a very fine model of the ancient fortress complete with its administrative buildings, its barracks, its walls and defences, its approach road, and much else. In show cases were shown weapons of all shapes and ages, seals and ivories, and much more than we could well take in during our brief visit. We walked over the great mound where the diggings had taken place, and admired the skill of the archaeologists in piecing together into a coherent story the evidence furnished by the twenty main occupation levels covering millenniums of time.

I had hoped to make contact with Dr Yadin, Israel's leading archaeologist at Megiddo, as I had brought with me to the Holy Land a letter of introduction to him, but I learned that he had returned to Jerusalem three days before our arrival. It would have been interesting to receive from him some account of his digs had he been on the spot. I have found his archaeological writings very rewarding.

*

We turned from Megiddo in the direction of Nazareth, recrossed the Plain of Esdraelon, and climbed the hills on its northern side. Nazareth we found rather disappointing, possibly because we were able to spend so little time there. It has increased so much in size of late years that it can bear little resemblance to the city of no reputation in which the Lord passed His childhood and His early manhood. As a small village it occupied 'a cup in the hills'; now a large city, it has broken its ancient bounds, and houses and premises of all kinds seem to be going up in profusion. Nazareth is now, in fact, two cities. Old Nazareth is almost predominantly Arab, and few Jews are found there; New Nazareth, overlooking Old Nazareth, is entirely Jewish, and the Arabs resent its establishment. The Jewish-Arab conflict finds unhealthy expression in the area. Hitherto the area in which Nazareth stands has been almost exclusively Arab: its inhabitants are aggrieved by the arrival of Jews who are much more progressive than themselves.

In Old Nazareth, as elsewhere, it was only too clear that ecclesiastical buildings which claimed to stand on particularly sacred spots completely obscured and blotted out everything that was realistic about them, and, as in Jerusalem, rendered them unnatural show places. That there were occasional gleams of architectural beauty is not to be denied, but it was our desire to see, not ornate domes and windows 'richly dight', but the simple, the homely and the true.

The Church of the Annunciation is built over the grotto where, according to tradition, the angel Gabriel visited Mary; the Church of St Joseph, rebuilt in the year 1914, contains ancient mosaics. The synagogue, supposedly occupying the site of the ancient synagogue where the Lord preached with *Isaiah* 61.1 as His text, and in consequence of which they endeavoured to cast him headlong from 'the brow of the hill on which their city was built', is attractive by virtue of its unmarred simplicity. In the synagogue a part of the sermon mentioned was read to us, with its mention of Naaman and the widow of Sarepta, 'Gentiles in the flesh'. Was it because of the Lord's introduction of these names that the intense and murderous hatred of the men of Nazareth was vented? The synagogue as a building possessed little inward or outward grace, but it was a most fitting place in which to listen to the searching teaching of 'the Word made flesh'. Joseph's workshop and the deep-down grotto where he and Mary lived were next shown to us. The grotto is at the end of a considerable descent and it is far from easy to convince oneself that the site is authentic. Tradition, even though ancient, may be sadly at fault.

Nazareth itself seemed to us to be unkempt, and as far as we saw it, uninviting, more akin to the 'back streets' of a western city than to main thoroughfares. There was a close resemblance to Jerusalem in its shops and workshops. Somehow carpenters' shops seemed to be specially abundant. Maybe our eyes were more alert for their presence than for other types of workshop. A narrow gutter ran down the centre of one of the streets through which we threaded our careful way, avoiding undue contact with the animals which passed by freely. Scraps of newsprint in Arabic and Hebrew were everywhere to be seen trodden under foot.

It was easy to suppose that as we stood in the streets of Nazareth we were looking upon a typical city of the Near East. Probably it is as proud today of its historic past as at one time it was ashamed of its ill reputation: 'Can any good thing come out of Nazareth?' But it illustrates that which God oft-times works with men: He brings the best out of the worst, the greatest good out of the greatest ill. 'He is wonderful in counsel and excellent in working' [*Isa.* 28.29].

Possibly my account of Nazareth renders it an injustice. Had we seen more of it we might have modified our opinion. Its setting in the hills was pleasant; its skies were blue; its limestone houses in some cases a delight to the eye; but above all else, one fact dimmed all others; here for thirty years lived in obscurity our Saviour and our Lord:

> '*We believe Thy footsteps trod*
> *Its streets and plains, Thou Son of God.*'

'He [Joseph] came and dwelt in a city called Nazareth, that it might be fulfilled which was spoken by the prophets, He shall be called a Nazarene' [*Matt.* 2.23].

The time factor was against us, so that we lacked opportunity to climb to higher ground than the city itself occupies and to take a view of the surrounding landscape. It may therefore be fitting to quote from the account given by Dr Edward Robinson aforementioned:

> *I walked out to the top of the hill over Nazareth. Here a glorious prospect opened on the view. The air was perfectly clear and serene; and I shall never forget the impression I received, as the enchanting panorama burst suddenly upon me. There lay the magnificent Plain of Esdraelon, or at least all its western part. On the left was seen the round top of Tabor over the intervening hills, with portions of the Little Hermon [another name for the Hill of Moreh mentioned in the history of Gideon: Jud. 7.1] and Gilboa and the opposite mountains of Samaria. Then came the long line of Carmel, with Haifa on the shore at its foot. In the west lay the Mediterranean, gleaming in the morning sun, seen first far in the south on the left of Carmel, then interrupted by that mountain, and again appearing on its right so as to include the whole Bay of Acre, Acre itself not being visible, being hidden by intervening hills . . . Carmel presented itself to great advantage, extending far out into the sea and dipping its foot in the waters.*
>
> *I remained for some hours upon this spot, lost in the contemplation of the wide prospect and of the events connected with the scenes around. In the village below, the Saviour of the world had passed His childhood . . . He must often have visited the fountain . . . His feet must frequently have wandered over the adjacent hills. His eyes doubtless have gazed upon the splendid prospect from this very spot. Here the Prince of Peace looked down upon the great plain, where the din of battles so oft*

had rolled, and the garments of the warrior been dyed in blood.
He looked out too upon that sea, over which the swift ships
were to bear the tidings of His salvation to nations and to
continents then unknown . . . and now the rays of that light
begin to be reflected back from distant isles and continents, to
illuminate anew the darkened land where it first sprung up.

*

From Nazareth we moved on to Mount Tabor, known to us
formerly merely as the reputed scene of the Transfiguration,
though some, with much more credibility, place that event on
one of the spurs of Mount Hermon. Tabor is the highest
mountain in Galilee, majestic on close acquaintance, though
described by a recent writer as 'not more than an overgrown
hillock'. It rises to about 1,800 feet, but it gains height, so to
speak, from the fact that it is not located on a ridge but rises
from the plain below in splendid isolation. Its summit is
rounded. Certain folk have conjectured that it is an extinct
volcano, but its geological characteristics – it is composed of
limestone – prove it to be simply 'a southern outcrop of the
Galilean hills', no more volcanic than are they. On the crest of
Tabor stands the Franciscan Church of the Transfiguration,
decorated with paintings of that event. In two side chapels are
paintings of Moses and Elijah respectively. A monk who acted
as guide inside the building read to us the Gospel narrative of
the Transfiguration in the Vulgate Version. I noticed that at the
entrance to the building was a notice which read: 'Women who
are immodestly dressed are forbidden to enter the monastery.'

Our ascent of Tabor was in two stages. The road which
circled its base halted at what seemed to be the half-way point
upwards, and we were transferred to waiting cars. Necessarily
so, for the rest of the journey was certainly adventurous.

Numerous hair-pin bends – the driver said there were 23 in all, but I myself lost count – took us along the edge of many precipitous descents until it seemed at times that there was 'but a step betwixt us and death'. But the drivers were skilled, as much so, we judged [though in a different line of things], as were certain men of Benjamin who, as recorded in *Judges*, could 'sling stones at an hair breadth, and not miss' [20.16]. Brakes, too, were good, so that in the good providence of God we made both ascent and descent in safety.

From the summit the view was superb, its beauty being enhanced by the historic character of the terrain on which we gazed. The Plain of Esdraelon is a chequerboard of pattern. It gave the impression that it is perhaps the most fertile and productive tilled land in Israel. Greens and browns of various shades resembled the lights and shadows which flicker over a landscape when the sunlight shines through broken cloud, except that the pattern was static. In the far distance, though still within the Plain, the agricultural colony of Nahalal appeared in its circular form as if it were a gigantic flower display in the public gardens of some great city. As from the hills above Nazareth where Dr Robinson made his observations, Carmel could be seen lifting its elongated head. The Kishon wandered across the Plain, seeking outlet in the Great Sea.

On the slopes of Tabor, Barak, one of the stalwarts of faith [*Heb.* 11.32], had mustered the host which attacked and overwhelmed Sisera, the captain of Jabin's army, as described in the *Book of Judges* [chapters 4 and 5]. It was not difficult to imagine the fierce fighting in the valley, 'in Taanach by the waters of Megiddo', 'the prancings of the mighty ones', the sudden rising of the Kishon, the flight of the foe before Israel, and the escape on foot of Sisera into the hills. Somewhere in the locality he was 'sold by the Lord into the hand of a woman'. 'So he died' runs the graphic biblical narrative. And overhead the stars in their courses had fought against him.

At the other end of the Valley Mount Gilboa was full in view. There King Saul and his three sons met their tragic end, an event which inspired David's generous lament: 'Ye mountains of Gilboa, let there be no dew, neither let there be rain, upon you, nor fields of offerings, for there the shield of the mighty is vilely cast away ... O Jonathan, thou wast slain in thine high places. I am distressed for thee, my brother Jonathan: very pleasant hast thou been unto me: thy love to me was wonderful, passing the love of women' [2 *Sam.* 1.21, 25, 26].

Not far away, across the valley from Gilboa and out of sight under the shadow of Tabor, lay Endor, the home of the witch consulted by Saul on the night before his death, an act which sealed his doom. It was not difficult to conceive of Saul, under cover of night, descending from the hills, and making his way stealthily across the plain to the strange encounter. Not far away, towards the Jordan, lay Bethshan. To its walls the head-less body of the king and the bodies of his sons were fastened by the Philistines. Some distance farther, beyond the Jordan, lay Jabesh-Gilead which had special cause to be grateful to the king for past help against Nahash, king of the Ammonites. Its men removed the bodies and gave them respectful burial. In a more westerly direction was Shunem, the home of the 'great woman' who entertained Elisha and met with great reward at his hands [2 *Kings* 4]. Historic ground indeed!

Beyond the Jordan the hills of Gilead, now known as the Hagolan Mountains, lift their crests and rolling uplands, gradu-ally merging into desert. To the North stretches once-populous Galilee, and beyond Galilee snowy Hermon. The Psalmist links Tabor and Hermon together in twin blessing: 'The

North and the South, Thou has created them. Tabor and Hermon shall rejoice in Thy Name' [89. 12]. Towards the North-east the end of the Sea of Galilee is visible, while the mountains of Syria in ever-increasing height form the horizon. Perhaps Mount Tabor is the best viewpoint in the whole of Palestine!

GALILEE

Blue as the Galilean lake,
Where the rent tower leans o'er the sunny wave
Which ripples round the ruined battlements
Of old Tiberias, and upon its bosom
Receives the shadow of these hanging palms,
The relics of a brighter, happier day,
When cities girdled all the smiling lake,
And gardens clad in glorious Syrian verdure
Clasped each fair city in their soft embrace.

ANON [from Lays of the Holy Land]

Further
Galilean
Joys

THE Lord's Day in Galilee brought its peculiar joys. It coincided with Whit Sunday in this instance. A party drawn
together on no other basis than a common desire to tour the
Holy Land will, understandably, consist of folk with a diversity
of opinions on spiritual matters. So far as a sight-seeing tour
is concerned, it is not difficult to make common cause, but
when matters involving the worship of God are involved,
groups tend to crystallize. Thus it was that conservative
evangelicals, led by the leader of the party, found themselves
on the Lord's Day morning in a small arched chapel, alcove-
shaped, a little way out of Tiberias and some five miles from
Ginosar, while those who wished to worship otherwise went
into Tiberias itself to an Anglican service. The small chapel
was attached to the local YMCA. Its aspect was towards the
sea. In the far distance Hermon raised its white peak. Three of
us – the leader [a Baptist minister], an Elim Pentecostalist, and
I [Free Church] took part in the service, the musical instru-
ment [a harmonium] being played by a member of the party
skilled in organ music. The message, by the first-mentioned,

was based upon Peter's preaching on the Day of Pentecost, and emphasized the basic content of the true Gospel of Christ.

In the afternoon a baptismal service was held in the grounds of our kibbutz, most of the members of our party being present. We sat on the shore of the Lake on stools which we carried from the roof of our hotel. A member of the party, we were informed, had been in communication with our leader about baptism earlier in the year, and had given him sound reason to conclude that she was a true believer. She by no means held the view that baptism in Galilee conveyed benefits above baptism in any other place, but had become persuaded that as a disciple of the Lord she must be immersed in the Triune Name, and this she conceived to be the fitting opportunity, the more so as she was not in a position in the homeland to apply to a minister holding Baptist principles.

The occasion was a very happy one. Those of us who took a share in carrying through the morning service were responsible for what was said and done, and the lady herself gave a testimony to the saving grace of God. Unexpectedly a few drops of rain fell at the outset, an unusual happening in mid-May, and heavy rolling clouds presaged a prospect of storm; but shortly the sun shone brightly again, and there was no hindrance. An appropriate word on the subject of baptism was ministered. We felt ourselves to be following in the direct succession of events in the Lord's own earthly ministry, and to be doing in 1967 what must have happened with great frequency in the first Christian century. The lady herself went on her way rejoicing, after the pattern set for her by a certain Ethiopian who similarly followed the Lord as he travelled along the highway from Jerusalem to Gaza.

In the evening the evangelicals gathered again on the roof of the hotel, sang hymns, listened to a short message based upon

four refusals linked with royalty – that of Moses when he refused to be called the son of Pharaoh's daughter, that of David
who refused to wear Saul's armour, that of Daniel when he
asked permission not to eat the king's meat, and that of the
Lord himself when he refused to accept the kingship offered to
Him by people assembled on the shores of Galilee. The crescent
moon shone in a cloudless sky above us, while 'silently, one by
one, in the infinite meadows of heaven, blossomed the lovely
stars, the forget-me-nots of the angels'. Two bright stars in
particular kept close company with the moon. A party of
Swedish Lutherans who occupied another part of the roof was
engaged similarly to ourselves, and after a time we joined forces
and sang together 'What a friend we have in Jesus', and 'How
great Thou art!' Whether our companion party sang in Swedish or in English I cannot say, but our voices seemed to blend
harmoniously together. At least one of the Swedish party
could converse in English, and though none of us could follow
suit in Swedish, one of us [the baptized lady] recited a Christian
verse in Swedish which memory brought back from earlier
years.

*

On the following day we resumed our tours of the Galilean
country. Northern Galilee is delightful in all directions. In days
when the tribal possessions were distinct, it was the territory
of Naphtali, Zebulun and Asher. Nowadays its chief centre is
Safad, the highest town of the province [2,750 feet], with a
most healthy climate. In the past it has been noted for its earthquakes, also for its rabbinical schools which gave it the character of a holy city. Particularly has it been famed for Cabbalistic
lore, that is to say, for secret tradition passed on by word of
mouth. Certain rabbis claimed that Moses had received it
[Kabbal=to receive] from God, and that it had been trans-

mitted orally across the centuries. Probably it originated in Babylon during the Captivity. It gave a mystical meaning, based in part upon the numerical value of letters, to every word and even to every letter of the Law, and substituted a kind of occultism for the plain and evident meaning of the Word of God. It was the enemy of the Gospel. In certain respects Safad was even a rival of Jerusalem. The city itself had a splendid setting in the hills. Early in the present century, if not earlier, it had a reputation for being 'extraordinarily dirty', but we had no opportunity or desire to form our own opinion on the matter. Our ignorance was our bliss.

We were cheered by seeing around us acres, if not square miles, of olive trees, and were reminded of the biblical statement to which I have already referred – 'Let Asher dip his foot in oil' [*Deut.* 33.24]. The blessing was fulfilled very agreeably before our eyes. We had been much pleased to find on sale in our kibbutz of Ginosar, postcards showing twelve Israeli postage stamps, each one depicting an emblem suited to the future history of the tribes as prophesied by Jacob or by Moses. Thus Judah was represented by a lion, Benjamin by a ravening wolf, Naphtali by a hind, Levi by a jewelled breastplate, Zebulun by a ship, and Asher by an olive tree. Our Israeli guide informed us that the use in Israel of olive oil [possibly he meant to indicate only oil of the best quality] was prohibited by the State, as it was all required for export to earn foreign currency. We judged that in northern Galilee the olive tree found a perfect environment: it could not have appeared more flourishing.

As we 'took our journey' we passed by a roadside shack where refreshments and a variety of knick-knacks were to be obtained, and were invited to walk round to its rear where, in the shelter of a wall, a woman was sitting on the ground 'baking cakes on the hearth', and as we watched we could well believe that the process had remained unchanged from time out of mind.

First, she sieved her flour, and quickly produced a small flat cake of unleavened dough, the size of a saucer. In the next stage of her art [for art it certainly was], she beat the cake with her hands until it had become as thin as a pancake, and in the process had necessarily become as large as a dinner plate, if not larger. This done, she took up the pancake, held it firmly in her right hand, and with remarkable deftness whirled it around with the left hand assisted by the right, until it could be seen visibly expanding to the size of a dust-bin lid. The action did not occupy more than a minute.

The woman then transferred the much-thinned-out cake to a padded cloth of similar size. Meanwhile by her side was an iron dome heated from below by a wood fire. Upon this by swift motion she slapped the cake and in a few moments it was baked. The heat of the dome caused the imprisoned air to expand and to produce a mass of small bubbles in the cake. We were invited to taste the finished product and found it quite appetizing, though we were not altogether convinced at heart that western hygiene had been fully respected in the various processes we had observed. But the woman's skill was pleasant to witness and we each rewarded her with a small coin.

Returning to the roadway we became engaged in a miniature battle carried on by contesting salesmen. It concerned baskets of similar make and size. Two Jewish teenage girls [I will imagine their names to be Miriam and Sarah] were keen to sell their wares to members of our party. A youth of about twelve years [I call him Aaron] was equally eager to develop pressure-salesmanship. With considerable difficulty a member of the party made her selection and attempted to open her purse to pay the favoured seller for it. Then ensued the battle royal. Sarah, and even more so Aaron, were still determined to press their wares. Baskets from three different quarters were pressed so close to the purchaser's hand that the extraction of coins from the purse proved almost impossible; until our more experienced leader, noting the trouble spot, came up with a suitable air of authority and rescued the lady from her embarrassing predicament. Miriam was given her due reward; her rivals reluctantly gave way; the waiting coach resumed its journey.

*

Nahariya on the coast, a little to the north of Acre [Acco] was our next place of call. It ranks as a holiday resort, has a delightfully sandy shore, and is much favoured by bathers. As it was Jewish Independence Day [15th May] the place was crowded with Israelis who were free from work, and we mingled with them on the shore, members of our party bathing or sitting on the sand as the mood seized them. We had been supplied by our hotel with a picnic lunch, so that apart from tea, coffee, or soft drinks we were virtually independent of restaurants. It only remains to add that access to the beach cost us 2s. per head.

After Nahariya and modernity, Acre and antiquity! Ominously in Scripture, the first mention of the place [*Judges* 1.31] tells us that Asher failed to fulfil the divine command to drive out the Canaanites who occupied it, though in later days there seems to have been a Jewish colony there. But in the eyes of the Greeks Acre belonged to Phoenicia rather than to Israel. It was called Ptolemais by one of the Ptolemies and is mentioned under that name in *Acts* 21.7. It owed its importance to its natural harbour and was used by the Crusaders as their chief port. In modern times it is chiefly remembered by Englishmen for its importance in stemming the onward march of Napoleon after he had conquered Egypt in 1798. He then advanced on Palestine and is even credited with the ambition to march through Syria and Asia Minor to Constantinople to overthrow the Turkish Empire. One of his battles was fought in the Plain of Esdraelon, after which he and his staff spent the night in a hospice at Nazareth. He next engaged in the siege of Acre, but it was defended by a young British naval officer, Sir Sydney Smith, and after nine weeks Napoleon had to admit defeat. A success which his forces had gained over the Turks at Mount Tabor was no compensation for the failure at Acre, and the great Frenchman abandoned what he now called 'the miserable little hole'. 'That man', he said of Smith, 'made me miss my destiny'.

We found Acre to be comparatively unimportant nowadays. Its harbour has been blocked by silt, and Haifa has replaced it as the great port of modern Israel through which all imports and exports pass. From one of the ancient forts we had an excellent view of the shore. If no longer of value to shipping, it is wonderfully colourful. Its shelving rocks, played upon by sunlight and lapped by white-capped waves, display all shades of green and blue. Such was their beauty that it was almost painful to break away from the site and to terminate the visit.

After Acre, Carmel! Haifa, the large and prosperous commercial and industrial city at the foot of Carmel we did not pause to inspect. After all, it is best seen from the heights at the base of which it spreads itself. It is not mentioned in Scripture. Carmel is a range rather than a mere headland. Solomon and Isaiah alike extol its beauty [*Song of Sol.* 7.5 and *Isaiah* 35.2: 'the excellency of Carmel']. Dr John Gill, in his commentary on the *Song of Songs*, remarks that the word 'Carmel' is sometimes used for green ears of corn [*Levit.* 2.14 and 23.14] and for a fruitful field as in *Isa.* 32.15. 'The word', he states, 'is by some rendered "crimson", and the rather, it may seem to be so taken in the *Song*, because *purple* is made use of in the next description [*Song* 7.5], and which go together, and are thus rendered, in 2 *Chron.* 2.7 and 3.14'.

Carmel is one of the land's limestone hills and gains fame from the fact that it is the most prominent feature of Israel's coastline, a kind of Palestinian Beachy Head. Also, and very unusually, it commonly remains green throughout the year on account of the heavy dews which distil upon it. On this mountain Elijah withstood the prophets of Baal in the reign of Ahab, and summoned the nation to return to the worship of Jehovah. Somewhere at its foot, where the Kishon flows, the false prophets were slain. On its crest the prophet put his face between his knees and prayed for the mercy-drops of blessing. Seven times his servant obeyed the word, 'Go up now and look toward the sea'. In God's good time came the little cloud out of the sea like a man's hand, after which came the deluge [1 *Kings* 18]. A man subject to like passions with us had 'prayed again, the heaven gave rain, and the earth brought forth her fruit' [*James* 5.18].

*

Cana of Galilee was visited during our return journey, after we had again passed through Nazareth and seen the Old and New City. Large indeed it seemed in its nest of hills. Cana in certain respects did not yield us much pleasure. Its inhabitants were sitting indolently along its narrow and none-too-clean streets and its children pestered our party for baksheesh. Cana was the only place in Israel where this happened to us. We entered the Franciscan Church which, it is claimed, is built on the site of the house where the marriage feast was held, as described in the second chapter of John's Gospel. Beneath its floor an attendant, lifting a trap-door, brought to view a mosaic which belonged to an earlier building on the site. Descending into an inner shrine we were shown a stone water-jar corresponding in size, we were told, to those in use when 'the conscious water saw its God, and blushed'. To most of us, however, its size appeared inadequate. A larger jar in an adjacent room seemed to correspond more nearly to the requirements of the miracle as described in Scripture.

It is often the case that the visitor takes with him to the various sites pre-conceived ideas of what he expects to see. Frequently his ideas call for considerable adjustment. But he tends to judge of the credibility of disputed sites by these notions. Alongside the jar just mentioned we were shown the mouth of a dry well, and were informed that in all probability this was the source from which the water which became wine was obtained. It had been in use until quite recently, when a more satisfactory source of water for the village was found.

Cana was the home of Nathanael. It is somewhat strange that John does not link Nathanael with Cana when he and Cana are introduced in the first and second chapters of his Gospel, but keeps back the information until the end of his *Gospel* [21.2]. Again, it was at Cana that the Lord spoke the word which healed the nobleman's son at Capernaum, some twenty miles away [*John* 4.46–54]. It only remains to add that scholars are in dispute about the location of Cana of Galilee, though all are agreed that it was not a great distance from Nazareth. The Cana which we visited, which appears to have the best claim of any to authenticity, is now known as Kefr Kenna and is on the road from Nazareth to Tiberias.

I have remarked on the persistence of children seeking baksheesh from visitors to Cana, and the following account of the way in which Dr W. H. Bartlett, a century ago, dealt with the problem is not without interest. It is taken from *Jerusalem Revisited* [1862]:

> *The women and children are often very troublesome, pestering the traveller for 'baksheesh' with a pertinacity that will accept no refusal. It was my fate to be thus surrounded, while drawing, by a group of black-eyed girls, some of whose faces, had they but been washed, might have been considered handsome, or at all events expressive. Some of them carried babies, of which, juvenile as was their appearance, they were most probably the mothers; and laughing all the while, studiously thrust the tattered clothing of their dirty infants into my very eyes, to create a feeling of sympathy. Annoyed at the interruption, I took at first no notice of them; whereupon they resorted to the most insinuating artifices – calling me, in Arabic, 'worthy Frank', patting me on the shoulder, ay, and even chucking me under the chin. I distributed two or three piastres among them, but this only served to draw down upon me a fresh set, until I suddenly bethought me of a very simple way to get rid of my persecutors. Fixing my eyes seriously upon one of the foremost girls, and then at my sketch-book, I pretended to be copying her lineaments, and thence glancing round at another, repeated the same manoeuvre. No sooner was my design perceived than it was comical to mark the expression of alarm that came gradually over their countenances, at what they evidently considered a magical operation; and stealing off one by one, in a very few moments they left me to finish my sketch without any further interruption.*

UNDER THE SHADOW OF HERMON

Here by Jordan's rushing waters
    Running free from Hermon's mount,
Where of old Dan's sons and daughters
    Often drank from sparkling fount.

See the Lord and His apostles
    For a time withdraw from men,
From the crowd which strives and jostles
    Just to touch His garment's hem.

Here Christ's face shines bright with glory,
    Brighter than the sun's bright beam,
While two named in ancient story
    With Him talk on Gospel theme.

'Exodus' from Salem's city
    Is their word for Jesus' death;
Peter [and we can but pity]
    Speaks out, too, but wastes his breath.

Cloud comes low, the sight concealing
    Now from Peter, James and John,
And a voice God's will revealing
    Falls from high their ears upon.

Clear and wondrous was the story –
    'Hear Him, my belovèd Son!'
[It was through Him, to God's glory
    That salvation must be won.]

Thus, the Father's will revealèd! –
    Brightest glory now must wane.
'Keep' said Christ, 'the scene concealèd,
    Till the day I rise again'.

From the mount they take their journey,
    Back again to realms of woe,
And the Subject of the glory
    Meets again His ancient foe.

Caesarea Philippi and the Syrian Border

O UR tours in Galilee were not yet completed. It remained to penetrate as far north as possible in the direction of Hermon, to the area where a part of the tribe of Dan was once located. Dan's allotment of land in the time of Joshua was in Central Palestine, west of the territory allocated to Benjamin. We are told, however [*Joshua* 19.47], that their 'coast went out too little for them', so that they were obliged to seek extension where they could best find it. They met with success in the far north, in land which seems to have belonged originally to the Zidonians [*Judges* 18]. Hence it was that the Israelites spoke of their land as stretching from Dan to Beersheba, the latter place denoting the limit of habitable land in the south before the Negev desert warns off all intruders into its pathless desolations.

Unhappily, the northern settlement of Dan commenced with an act of gross idolatry, and later Jeroboam 1 set up there his calf worship [as also at Bethel: 1 *Kings* 12.29]. To Dan's link with idolatry some ascribe the absence of the name of Dan from the twelve tribes named in the seventh chapter of *Revelation*.

If the supposition is correct, we have an illustration of the principle that, while those who honour the Lord will be honoured by Him, those who despise Him are lightly esteemed [1 *Sam.* 2.30].

From Ginosar we headed northwards, therefore, and soon found ourselves in the fertile strip of country bounded on the west by the mountains of Naphtali and on the east by those of Golan and Bashan in Syria. There was every indication that this particular territory was fertile and productive. It is watered by the Jordan flowing down from the base of snowy Hermon. Until recent years much of the land was swampy, especially around the Waters of Merom, latterly called Lake Huleh. In consequence of this malaria was prevalent, but not long ago the Lake was drained, the land reclaimed and planted, and the dreaded scourge has been completely eliminated. The land has been planted with lemons, grapefruit, and other fruits, also with such crops as groundnuts. Some years ago it was estimated that ten million dollars' worth of food could be produced by the area annually. Until it was drained the lake frequently overflowed and inundated the low-lying fields around it. That is now remedied, to the advantage not only of the territory of Naphtali, but of the whole land of Israel.

Our immediate interest was to attain a sight, as nearly as could be, of Caesarea Philippi just over the Syrian border. This has been one of the trouble spots in Syro-Israeli relations, and the United Nations has maintained an observation post there for several years. We could see it in the distance. Our eyes were also directed to certain markings on the hillside in front of us which, we were informed, represented attempts made by Syria about three years ago to divert the waters of the Jordan away from Israel. The effort proved unsuccessful and had been abandoned. At this point both sides of the unseen frontier were jealously guarded by troops which we could not see, but which doubtless kept watch on our peaceful activities. Thus our information ran!

According to ancient pagan tradition, a grotto in the area, from which the Jordan emerged, was a sanctuary of the Greek god Pan. Herod the Great decided to erect a marble temple at the spot in honour of his patron, the Roman Emperor Augustus. The place was further developed by Philip the Tetrarch, one of Herod's sons, and it was he who named it Caesarea Philippi to distinguish it from Caesarea on the Palestinian coast. It is also recorded that, after the fall of Jerusalem in AD 70, the Emperor Titus celebrated his victory by holding gladiatorial combats here, though he appears to have done a similar thing in other cities too. The chief interest of Christians in the site derives from the fact that Christ visited it. It was here that he questioned the disciples about His Messiahship, and here that Peter made the great confession, 'Thou art the Messiah, the Son of the living God' [*Matt.* 16.13–16]. Here, too, therefore that the words were spoken on which the Roman Church wilfully bases its arrogant claims. The contention that the Transfiguration occurred in this area rather than on Mount Tabor is based on the near connection of the Transfiguration narrative in the Synoptic Gospels with the events at Caesarea Philippi [*Matthew*, chapters 16 and 17; *Mark*, chapters 8 and 9; *Luke*, chapter 9].

We duly reached Kibbutz Dan and to our amazement were ushered into a fine building of recent construction named Beit Ussishkin [House of Ussishkin]. It is the Institute of Natural History of the Huleh Valley. Menachem Ussishkin, who died in 1941 at the age of 78, had been a prominent worker for the Zionist Movement, and the Institute is his memorial. Its declared aims are 'to study the flora and fauna of the valley, to acquire and preserve all material on the national history of the area and its settlement from the earliest times, and to propagate this knowledge among the public and among school-children and youth in particular'. The Institute includes a large Lecture Hall in which we seated ourselves to listen to a tape-recorded address of welcome. Chairs had arms, but the right-hand arm was flat and wide, after the style of an artist's palette, but larger, and designed to enable the student to rest his note-book upon it. It obviated the need for a separate student's desk. We were impressed. The exhibits were excellently arranged and were as good as, if not better than those seen in our largest cities. All were excellently mounted and displayed to maximum advantage. All members of our party were impressed by the skill of those responsible for the Institute; and our amazement was the greater when we considered that the building seemed so remote from any considerable centres of population. It was an essentially rural area and the various kibbutzim were widely scattered.

*

We next undertook a brief tour of the area adjacent to the Institute, in which the Jordan takes its rise. It was an enjoyable adventure. Most rivers have more than one stream which can be designated 'source' and this holds good of the Jordan. Dependable maps show four such streams, of which the most easterly is the most famous. It is known as the Banias, a corruption of the name Paneion, or sanctuary of Pan. J. Howard Kitchen in his book, *Holy Fields* [1955], writes thus of it:

> *Here from a cavern lying at the base of a high cliff stained red with rust rushes out full-fledged a stream of sparkling water fully thirty feet broad. Flowing at first through a deep gorge spanned by an ancient Roman Bridge, it later passes through pleasant meadows and tree-lined slopes on its way to join the Jordan.*

That the flow was indeed copious we tested for ourselves, for as we walked along a slippery, winding and rugged path through the shrubs and low trees which overhung it, we had to cross perhaps fifteen sets of stepping stones, all set amid currents of swift-running water. Such was its abundance, it might have been supposed that heavy rains contributed regularly to the flow. We knew the case to be far otherwise. And yet, that very day, we had experienced an afternoon of rain, a most unusual happening [so we were assured] in the month of May. Our coach was fitted with a radio, but as its news was in Hebrew it was lost upon us. On the return journey, however, our Jewish guide informed us that it had just announced a torrential downpour in the Negev which had resulted in the temporary blocking of the road to Eilat at the head of the Gulf of Akaba. We were not altogether surprised that one of the windscreen wipers on the coach refused to work. Little-used apparatus is apt to function badly.

I returned from the Banias with a cluster of first-ripe figs plucked from a tree overhanging the stream; also with admiration for the achievement which was turning an area of formerly pestilential swamp into a land of abundant fruitfulness. The sight of a fox which crossed our pathway as we turned again southwards suggested that the members of the kibbutzim in the district might still find it necessary to exhort one another in the ancient words: 'Take us the foxes, the little foxes, that spoil the vines: for our vines have tender grapes' [*Song of Sol.* 2.15].

*

On the outward journey we had passed by an ancient 'tell', the site of Hazor, which, in the time of Joshua, was the chief Canaanitish stronghold in upper Galilee. We are told that Joshua destroyed it, but Scripture gives little information about the exploit. Professor Garstang identified the site in 1926 and thirty years later Dr Yadin of Jerusalem undertook the first major dig there. Hazor proved to be the largest city in the Holy Land in the time of the conquest by Joshua; Scripture itself says so [*Josh.* 11.10] and the archaeologist merely confirms the statement. Dr Yadin sent a detailed account of his work to the *Illustrated London News* during 1958 and in the issue dated 19 April of that year he says:

> *Holding the Bible in one hand and a spade in the other seemed to be a most successful method for discovering the relics of this biblical city and determining their dates. Thus, for example, the fact that Solomon rebuilt Hazor and Megiddo* [1 Kings 9.15] *was not only strikingly confirmed in this year's dig, but also enabled us to outline in advance on the surface the plan of Solomon's city gate by simply copying that of the gate discovered in Megiddo some years back. When finally the gate at Hazor was revealed and actually turned out as expected, our labourers thought we were wizards.*

It was in this dig that Dr Yadin, assisted by Scripture, found ways and means of dating certain pottery with accuracy, an all-important matter for the archaeologist. We cannot enter here into detailed explanations; the following words, also written by Dr Yadin, are, however, worth quoting:

> *One of our most cherished hopes was that the dig at Hazor might reveal the date of Joshua's destruction of the city and so help us to fix the date of the Exodus, one of the most vexed problems among biblical scholars.* Joshua 11.10–11 *says that Joshua took Hazor, then the head of all the surrounding kingdoms, and burnt it with fire. This Canaanite city when found, was the biggest in size discovered in the Holy Land, as was appropriate to 'the head of all these kingdoms'* [*it was fifteen*

times bigger than Jerusalem in David's time]. Its pottery consisted of the famous Mycenaean imported ware [that is, from the Aegean islands] of the 13th century BC. This was decisive proof that the main phase of the conquest of Canaan took place about 1240 BC the date which scholars suggested long ago but which could not previously be proved.

And yet another quotation from the same writer in reference to the importance of Hazor's mound as it threw light on matters of a date long subsequent to Joshua's day:

While clearing the remains of City Six [below the remains of the city destroyed by the Assyrian Tiglath Pileser] we noticed that, in contrast with remains above it, it bore no trace of destruction by man. No traces of fire; and most of all the household pottery was in situ. On the other hand, the walls of the houses, their columns, and so on, were found tilted. The only logical conclusion was that the city had been destroyed by earthquake. But when? Obviously before 732 [the date of Tiglath Pileser]. Moreover the pottery indicated that it was flourishing during the eighth century. Now the Bible is rich in information about cities destroyed by conquest. But earthquakes? Imagine our joy when in the first verse of Amos we read, 'The words of Amos . . . which he saw concerning Israel in the days of Uzziah king of Judah, and in the days of Jeroboam . . . two years before the earthquake'. Jeroboam reigned in Judah some fifteen years before Pekah [who was overthrown by Tiglath Pileser [2 Kings 15.29]. Thus we could fix the date of destruction of City Six.

Unhappily our visit to Hazor was of the most fleeting character. In fact it was not really a visit at all, for we lacked the time to halt at the 'tell' and would have passed it by altogether, but the guide and driver of our coach paused for three brief minutes to allow me to ascend the near part of the ruins and to select a stone as a memorial of my visit. The stone is duly labelled 'Hazor'.

And so, back to the lowlands of Galilee!

*

Now had come the day of our return flight to England. To reach Lod [Lydda] Airport, near Tel Aviv, early in the day, in readiness for the flight, it was necessary for us to rise at about 4 AM. After a light breakfast we left Ginosar by coach [there are railways in the Holy Land but they count for very little] and arrived at the Airport by 8.30. The journey by air was uneventful. Its chief interest was in the views it occasionally granted us over very extensive territories, though the first part of the journey was of course over the Mediterranean and the Adriatic. Unfortunately there was much cloud and for the greater part of the trip we could see little but the white billowy blanket beneath the plane. Now and again, through breaks in the cloud, we caught glimpses of historic lands, here and there an island, once or twice a ship. I outlined on paper, with such detail as I could manage, the coastline of one of the larger islands in the hope that, by comparison later with a map, I might be able to ascertain its name; but I failed to solve the conundrum. Now and again we saw a mountainous terrain with grey serpentine roads marked out clearly in the valleys. One Alpine peak only pierced the clouds; was it Mount Blanc? We could not tell. France too was largely blotted from sight, but breaks in the cloud-cover occasionally revealed the pattern of fields. Squares, rectangles, parallelograms, rhombuses, trapeziums all seemed to contribute their shapes to the intricate lay-out below. We hardly knew when we were crossing the Channel or were within sight of the white cliffs. Strangely, there was much less cloud over England than elsewhere, and green fields seemed to stretch away into far distances. Jordan's sandy wastes and Israel's vines and olives were far removed in time and place, but we carried them, so to speak, on our hearts. Then Gatwick appeared in sight. The touch-down was perfect. Customs and other formalities occupied but a few minutes, and shortly the company had scattered to its various destinations. The non-stop journey from the Holy Land had taken a little over seven hours.

*

When a tour ends, memory begins its pleasing work. It was good in anticipation; it is better still in retrospect to have in view the

> *'holy fields*
> *Over whose acres walked those blessed feet*
> *Which . . . were nailed*
> *For our advantage to the bitter cross.'*

Certainly the Christian stands in need of no mere territorial tour in order to enter into the full enjoyments of his 'most holy faith'. But whereas Isaac Watts could, in his day, wistfully say, 'Could I but climb where Moses stood, and view the landscape o'er', modern modes of communication have translated the elusive hopes of an eighteenth-century day into vivid twentieth-century realization; and the earthly land which was formerly 'very far off' has come within six or seven hours' journey.

It is good, where the opportunity presents itself, to set eyes on the land of which Scripture declares that 'the eyes of thy God are always upon it from the beginning of the year unto the end of the year'. Strange has been its history and changed is its present character. But to multitudes it has been and remains a land unique, a land of events unparalleled in human story, a land blessed, a land cursed, a land which in the most vital of all matters remains earth's centre, even as its capital remains earth's central city.

The Christian's faith is not confined within a geographical and historical context, any more than his devotions are confined to his 'place of worship', but it is linked with such a context. The 'holy city' of earth pictures the 'city which has foundations, whose builder and maker is God'; the 'holy land' shadows the 'better country, that is, an heavenly'. In a very real sense the history and geography of the 'land of promise' are alike parabolic. Happy are they who can find 'tongues in trees, books in the running brooks, and sermons in stones' in the Palestinian scene.

As for Israel, now settled again in its land, though at present in unstable equilibrium, much of prophetic Scripture bears upon its past, its present and its future. I close my narrative with verses which, in my view, put the problem into its biblical setting. A holy land and a holy city demand a holy people. 'Holiness to the Lord' must needs pertain to the very bells of the horses, and to the pots and bowls in the Lord's house. And above all, 'in that day there shall be no more the Canaanite in the house of the Lord of hosts' [*Zech.* 14.21].

*

I would not, brethren, that ye should be ignorant of this mystery, lest ye should be wise in your own conceits; that blindness in part is happened to Israel, until the fulness of the Gentiles be come in.

And so all Israel shall be saved: as it is written, There shall come out of Sion the Deliverer, and shall turn away ungodliness from Jacob:

For this is my covenant unto them, when I shall take away their sins.

As concerning the gospel, they are enemies for your sakes: but as touching the election, they are beloved for the fathers' sakes. For the gifts and calling of God are without repentance.

.   .   .

O the depth of the riches both of the wisdom and knowledge of God! how unsearchable are His judgments, and His ways past finding out!

For who hath known the mind of the Lord? or who hath been His Counsellor?

Or who hath first given to Him, and it shall be recompensed unto Him again?

For of Him, and through Him, and to Him, are all things: to whom be glory for ever. Amen. [Romans 11. 25–36]

ISRAEL

Israel blessed and Israel banished,
    Israel chastened and restored
Is one theme of Holy Scripture –
    She is loved who was abhorred.

Everlasting love and blessing
    Is her portion from the Lord;
'For the fathers' sakes beloved'
    Runs the true and faithful word.

She's the olive tree God planted,
    Stock of Abraham called from far,
Fenced around and digged and watered,
    Nought can injure her or mar.

Also to the vine comparèd,
    In a very fruitful hill;
But when grapes should be the vintage,
    Wild grapes all the vineyard fill.

And when Christ came forth to bless her,
    Son of Husbandman was He,
' 'Tis the heir', men said together,
    'All His words are vanity.'

'And His works', they said, 'are evil;
    He is fit to die the death;
How can good to Jewish people
    Come from out of Nazareth?'

'Crucify Him, crucify Him',
    Raise Him high on cross of wood;
Vilify Him, scorn His doctrine,
    From Him there can come no good.'

Thus they treated Christ the Saviour,
    Venting on Him all their spite.
Stricken then were they with blindness,
    While to Gentiles comes the light.

Israel's city next was trodden
    Underneath the conqueror's heel;
Fulness of the Gentiles only
    Can make woe give place to weal.

Branches broke from Jewish olive –
    Unbelief is dire disgrace –
And instead were Gentile peoples
    Grafted in to take their place.

But the Lord whose heart is mercy,
  Graft them in again can He,
Take away their sin and bring them
  Back into His family.

At His advent out of Zion
  He will all the nations shake;
Then His Israel shall be savèd,
  Loved are they for fathers' sake.

Nothing can His cov'nant cancel,
  Nought there is in Heaven or Hell
Can persuade Him to repent of
  Promised good to Israel.

Pray we for this ancient people,
  'Everlasting nation' they;
If their fall brought Gentiles blessing,
  How much more in that glad day

Will their wondrous restoration
  Bring to men riches of grace,
In a measure none have witnessed
  Since the sun began its race!

                                SMH

Indexes

[209]

Jaffa Gate (Jerusalem) 137
Jebus 49, 59
Jebusites 50, 52, 53, 54, 55, 57
Jephthah 28
Jeremiah 14, 49
Jericho 44, 47, 52, 105, 106, 109, 115, 117–121, 123, 127–129
Jeroboam I (King) 85, 87, 193
Jerome 102
Jerusalem 26, 27, 34–37, 39, 41–80, 81, 95, 96, 97, 98, 102, 103, 105, 117, 127, 135–139, 140, 144, 146, 148, 156, 173, 195
Jethro 163
Jezreel, Valley of, 169
Joab 28, 54, 55, 103, 104
Job's Well 49, 51
John the Baptist 33, 90, 139, 142
Johnson, Samuel (USA) 34
Jonathan 136, 179
Jordan (River) 19, 32–33, 36, 41, 47, 113, 116, 120, 122–123, 194, 196–197
(State of) 20, 25–26, 134
Joseph (son of Jacob) 85, 104
(of Arimathaea) 70, 71
(husband of Mary) 172, 174
Josephus 50, 51, 102, 140, 142, 147
Joshua 32, 48, 50, 83, 85, 118, 120–121, 136, 170, 193, 197, 198
Josiah (King) 49, 170

Judah 184
Julius Caesar 141

Kaaba 68
Kedar 31
Kefr Kenna 189
Kenyon, Kathleen 118, 123
Kibbutzim 145, 161–162
Kidron 41, 42, 46, 49, 50, 51, 62, 74, 78, 89, 137
King's Highway 106
Kirjath-jearim 151
Kishon (River) 169, 176, 188
Kitchen, J. Howard 196
Knesset 135, 137
Knox, John 16
Koran 91, 105

Lays of the Holy Land 179
Lazarus (of Bethany) 96–97
League of Nations 25, 26
Lejjun 170
Levi 184
Livy 14
Lloyd George, D. 136
Lod (Lydda) 200
Lomond, Loch 155
London 13, 34, 43, 69, 119
Lord's Day services 79, 181–183
Lot 26
Lot's wife 126, 127
Lynch, Lieut 126

Maan 107
Macalister, R. A. Stewart 53, 54
Machaerus 90, 142
Machpelah 104

PAPERBACKS

An Alarm to the Unconverted: *Joseph Alleine*
160 *pages*, 4s 6d

*The Christian View of Man: *J. Gresham Machen*
240 *pages*, 5s

Five Christian Leaders: *J. C. Ryle*
192 *pages*, 4s 6d

For a Testimony: *Bruce F. Hunt*
160 *pages*, *illus*, 5s

The Forgotten Spurgeon: *Iain Murray*
224 *pages*, 5s

*Genesis 3: *Edward J. Young*
176 *pages*, 5s

*God-Centred Evangelism: *R. B. Kuiper*
240 *pages*, 6s

Heaven on Earth: *Thomas Brooks*
320 *pages*, 5s

Human Nature in its Fourfold State: *Thomas Boston*
480 *pages*, 10s 6d

The Life of M'Cheyne: *Andrew Bonar*
192 *pages*, 3s 6d

*Redemption Accomplished and Applied: *John Murray*
192 *pages*, 3s

The Rich Man and Lazarus: *Brownlow North*
128 *pages*, 3s 6d

The Sovereignty of God: *A. W. Pink*
160 *pages*, 2s 6d

A Summary of Christian Doctrine: *Louis Berkhof*
192 *pages*, 3s 6d

Not available to USA or Canada

THE GENEVA SERIES OF COMMENTARIES

OTHER TITLES

Andrew Bonar: Diary and Life
552 pages, 15s

The Christian in Complete Armour: *William Gurnall*
1200 pages, 35s

The Confession of Faith: *A. A. Hodge*
430 pages, 15s

George Whitefield's Journals
596 pages, illus, 25s

Men of the Covenant: *Alexander Smellie*
660 pages, illus, 21s

The Reformers and the Theology of the Reformation:
William Cunningham
624 pages, 30s

The Religious Affections: *Jonathan Edwards*
382 pages, 15s

Simon Peter: *Hugh Martin*
160 pages, 12s 6d

Spurgeon: the Early Years
470 pages, 21s

*Systematic Theology: *Louis Berkhof*
784 pages, 30s

*Thy Word is Truth: *E. J. Young*
280 pages, 15s

*

For free illustrated catalogue please write to
THE BANNER OF TRUTH TRUST
78b Chiltern Street London w1